Contents

In Search of Learning

A New Approach to School Management

Marter

Blackwell Education

First published 1990

© Marten Shipman 1990

Published by Basil Blackwell Ltd
108 Cowley Road
Oxford OX4 1JF
England

British Library Cataloguing in Publication Data
Shipman, M. D. (Marten Dorrington) *1926–*
    In search of learning: a new approach to school management.
    1. Great Britain. Schools. Management
    I. Title
    371.2'00941

    ISBN 0–631–16835–4
    ISBN 0–631–16836–2 pbk

Typeset in 10 on 11½ Garamond by Photo·graphics, Honiton, Devon.
Printed in Great Britain by T. J. Press (Padstow) Limited.

Introduction

Learning is the business of schools. It should be the priority for school management. Yet it is usually ignored in school management training. Means have got confused with ends.

The confusion of means and ends also accounts for the tedium in books and courses on school management. The excitement in schools is not around the routine administration usually discussed, but around learning. That is where teachers develop their own styles and adjust the National Curriculum to their children and their local circumstances. The neglect of learning has robbed management training not only of its rationale, but of its interest. Even more important, it has deflected attention away from the bottom-up enterprise which has developed education in the past, which remains the condition for success in the future and which is assumed in the 1988 Education Reform Act.

These are the major themes of this book. Because it is in the learning situation that teachers take the lead and interact with colleagues, pupils and parents, there is the opportunity to make management training both better informed and less boring. The evidence on successful teaching and learning, on successful curriculum development and effective school organisation has been largely ignored. That evidence is not only informative but entertaining. This is an appeal for more effective and more modern management training, for a sunrise not a sunset style and for a few more laughs. Fortunately they all come together.

The most successful headteacher I ever met could not even manage to match his own socks. Twenty years later I realise that he was practising what is now the technique favoured by hi-tech industry, MBWA, Management By Wandering Around (Peters and Austin, 1985). The staff fizzed with ideas and parents queued to get a place for their children. The LEA were proud of its achievements even if inspectors despaired of his paperwork. As I read books on school management I picture those odd socks and the pottering about. But I also remember his concern with learning, the efficiency of senior staff, the concern with standards among teachers and that I was there to help establish effective evaluation to inform teachers, pupils and parents.

Early in the study of school organisation I investigated a contrasting school (Shipman, 1971). This was described as a 'tight ship' by LEA inspectors. It had a strong senior management team. Students on teaching practice were given a manual of job specifications. Parents were given a prospectus detailing objectives and procedures. Yet in the school were listless children and bored staff. They were organised like battery hens. Parents tried to send their children elsewhere. The headteacher was rarely seen around the school. Learning seemed to be incidental.

This is not an argument against effective school management. That was needed in the expansive days of the 1960s and still is, following the 1988 Education Reform Act. I am arguing about the *focus* of effective school management. The safest bet for parents with limited knowledge of schools is to pick the one that at least seems to know where it is going and makes public how it intends to get there. But management is more than administration. The real difference between the two schools above was that the former was directly concerned with learning, the latter only indirectly. In the former, information was spread wide, focused on learning and the main purpose of the wandering of the head. In the latter, information was controlled by the 'senior management team' and never seen as the key to empowering others to raise attainment. Means here had got confused with ends.

The mechanistic, battery-hen model of schooling deals with procedures out of the context of schools as complicated social organisations set up to promote learning. It can be seen in many books published as school management became a national priority for the in-service education of teachers in the mid-1980s. Most of these books and the courses that use them are humane, practical, based on experience and designed to help senior staff run schools effectively. They met an urgent need for advice among teachers thrust into managerial positions without preparation. They have come from serving teachers (see for example, Blatchford, 1985), from inspectors (see for example, Felsenstein, 1987), from academics (see for example Day *et al*, 1986), from industrialists looking at schools (see for example, Everard, 1986), and from business school (see for example Handy, 1984). Most important of all were the publications of the National Development Centre for School Management Training (NDC) set up to produce models for management training development (see for example, McMahon and Bolam, 1987).

The dates of these books listed above are significant. They are all pre-1988 and hence have been overtaken by the Education Reform Act of that year. But the approach has not changed in books designed for the implementation of the Act. These still tend to deal with specific aspects such as the National Curriculum and local financial management as if they were isolated developments (see for example, Emerson and Goddard, 1989; Oldroyd and Caldwell, 1988). In practice, these developments and the changed political balance between teachers and parents are closely connected. They call for a synoptic, whole-school approach to school management focused on raising standards of attainment for all children. That is the rhetoric of the 1988 Act as well as the teachers' motivation. Further, the Act is only one move in a wide-ranging reform of public services. It would be ironic if an Act designed to move the education service into the enterprise culture was implemented by giving priority to management training that inhibited initiative. It would also be macabre if an Act justified as a way of raising standards led to priorities in management training which still ignored the learning that is the reason for spending £20 billion a year on the education service. There is a need to turn school management training upside-down so that bottom-up enterprise becomes a downhill task.

1 Management for learning

Schools exist to promote learning. That is also the end of management. Each school should have a curriculum that 'promotes the spiritual, moral, cultural, mental and physical development of pupils'. That was established in the Education Act of 1944. It is extended in the 1988 Education Reform Act to include preparation for 'the opportunities, responsibilities and experiences of adult life'. It is a tough as well as vague assignment. Learning is individual and children are a varied lot. We know little about how they learn or the best way to help them. We argue over the curriculum and find it difficult to agree whether learning should be child- or teacher-centred. It is difficult to sort out the influence of schooling from that of family and community. Yet these difficulties are not excuses for writing about school management as if it had no end beyond the establishment of efficient routines.

The problem can be seen in the topics recommended for school management training. Here is a typical list of courses for school management organised by a local education authority. It includes pastoral care, policy making, financial planning and control, personnel management, staff selection and appraisal, negotiation, management structures, delegation, accountability, team building, administrative procedures and responsibilities, conditions of service, health and safety, disciplinary procedures, grievance procedures, relations with governors, relations with parents and curriculum development. Even curriculum development, the one course that is close to learning, is about organisation, not elements of learning and characteristics such as breadth and balance, progression and continuity spelled out as crucial by HMI (DES, 1985a). No doubt attendance did improve the quality of schooling. But raised attainment would have been incidental. The list and its descriptions of courses is totally about means apparently unrelated to ends.

The 1988 Education Reform Act, as with the *Better Schools* policy (DES, 1985b and 1986) and the HMI *The Curriculum from 5 to 16* series (DES, 1985a) that preceded it, focused attention firmly on higher attainment as the goal. The National Curriculum, its assessment and the measures to make schools accountable for the learning achieved, strengthen the link between the ends and means of schooling, tighten the structure and increase the provision of information on learning for parents. Management training has been given the task of improving teaching quality and of raising attainment. These moves make the criticisms in this chapter more important. Schools should promote learning. So should management. Yet learning is rarely mentioned in books, articles and courses. These were already redundant in 1988. Those produced since are repeating the same old mistake. They are still confusing means and ends.

The difficulty for management training in education lies partly in the nature of schools as organisations. They can be boring or exciting, traditional or progressive, efficient or chaotic and it can still be difficult to separate the effective from the weak when learning is in focus. This is not just due to the effects of contrasting environments on children. Each has its own history, its own catchment area, its own staff. The interest of teachers lies primarily in the successes and failures of their pupils. Teaching skills are largely employed in allocating time and energy to improve curriculum, pedagogy, human relationships and attainment in the classroom. It is there that new ideas are generated. It is where the pain and joy are felt. School management training tends to operate above this bustle of ideas. It misses most of the fun, many of the ideas and the grip of the drama where learning is promoted or frustrated. Teachers have their own ideas on how things should be run. This isn't cussedness. It is legitimate, responsible professional practice. Indeed, it is teachers who neglect to think through to a position where the children are getting the most out of work who are culpable. There is then a need to probe into the difficulties faced by those who want to help in improving school management.

The trouble with contemporary school management training

1 *The lack of concern with learning*
The reasons for the neglect of learning in management training include the following related factors.

a *The claim to professional autonomy*
The task of management training is made more difficult by the exclusiveness of classrooms. Teachers are organising their work within the framework of the National Curriculum and its assessment. Yet the way they teach is their business. Hence there is reluctance to touch learning in school management training. It can be seen as an attack on professional autonomy, beyond the responsibilities of headteacher and senior staff. Even where teachers are gathered together to develop school management, they tend to avoid the question at the heart of schooling, 'is the quality of teaching good enough?'. Most in-service training flirts around but does not touch this sensitive issue.

In practice, school management is always concerned with the allocation of resources for learning. Local financial management only makes that more apparent in schools. Management has also to ensure that teachers have an environment in which learning can take place. Teachers have also always been appraised, if only when they applied for other posts. The reluctance of headteachers and other senior staff to go into classrooms to observe teaching is an indication of the difficulties raised by the claim to professional autonomy. School management training still reflects this reluctance. Consequently it can avoid problems right at the heart of the school instead of addressing them.

b *The specialisation in the social sciences*
The interest of psychologists in the learning process, of sociologists in the human relations in schools, of political scientists in the distribution of power and of management theorists in models of organisations rarely overlap. Management theory is specialised. It grew through the study of organisations, particularly in industry. Its concern is usually at the macroscopic

level, with structure and culture, with resources, with relationships. There have been attempts to use psychology, but these
have rarely been followed up (see for example Simon, 1945).
Similarly, the insights of sociology into the different meanings
that are given to the same events in organisations tend to be
ignored. Thus management training tends to be severed from
social sciences that could provide the information to connect
it to learning and its social conditions. The relevant evidence
is presented in Chapters 5, 6 and 7.

c   *Teaching and learning are not readily managed*
It is difficult for management to get beyond establishing a
context for learning to take place. It cannot be too intrusive.
Learning is essentially individual. The teacher can teach, but
some children won't learn. Others seem to require little teaching. Further, the reasons why children learn and the way they
learn are not fully understood. Nor is there a strong tradition
of pedagogy, the principles and methodology of teaching, in
Britain. Thus management can provide a context for learning,
can ensure that it is given priority, can obtain cohesion and
continuity between teachers, can establish assessment, reporting and feedback arrangements. These are still rare in management training. They don't guarantee success. They are time-
consuming and politically sensitive.

We do know however that it has been very difficult to
uncover evidence that schools have major effects once the
social background of children is taken into account (see for
examples Rutter, 1979 and Mortimore, 1988). The most
reliable conclusion is that schools account for the progress of
children, but their attainment is heavily influenced by factors
outside. Thus schools may work wonders with children who
nevertheless perform at a low level because of external factors.
Other schools do a mediocre job in progressing children, but
they perform at a high level because of support in family
and community. This means that there is little incentive to
concentrate on learning. It can appear to be too dependent on
external and hence unmanageable factors. Yet as children learn,
internal and external factors are inseparable. In primary
schools the lesson has often been learned and parents are
increasingly involved in early reading and mathematics. In
secondary schools parents are, for better or worse, getting

involved in GCSE coursework. But the tradition of exclusion remains strong and is built into most books and courses on school management. External influences are only rarely treated as potentially supportive.

2 Schools are different

Recommendations for the management of schools are influenced by the success of methods developed elsewhere. That is legitimate. Schools have a lot in common with other service organisations. But it is necessary to be cautious. Schools are often likened to 'total institutions', a term coined by Goffman (1961) after a study of asylums. Evidence is borrowed from studies of prisons, hospitals, factories, offices and armies. Morgan (1986) has detailed many metaphors used in studying organisations. Looking at a school as a machine, a building, an organism, a brain and so on can lead to insights about how things work. But there are aspects of schooling which call for a bespoke approach. To take management theories off the peg, or not to appreciate that even practical tips for teachers contain implicit models of the school, is perilous.

Many books on school management list the differences between schools and other organisations on which management theories have been developed. This has been particularly popular among those looking at schools from their experience in industry (see for example Everard, 1982). These differences are easy to list. But they often neglect to list the failures and follies of industry and office. Most organisations have unclear goals and difficulties over the means of achieving them. The important difference is that schools exist to promote learning and this leads to a problem in the availability of information for making decisions.

Victorians had no doubts about the aim of elementary schools to get the children off the streets. But any contemporary attempt to spell out aims runs into problems over those 'spiritual, moral, cultural, mental and physical' qualities. Supporters of home economics, personal and social education, pastoral care, multi-cultural education, sociology and so on appeal to these qualities to defend their space on the timetable. But all organisations have entrenched interests appealing to unclear goals. It is very difficult to know whether prisons are aimed at reform, deterrence or retribution or even producing more crafty and informed criminals. The health service has no clear policy over its priority to prevent or cure illness. Private industry is often confused. Maximising profits is a clear aim, but at the expense of the environment? By forcing down wages? By selling to anyone, anywhere regardless of national interest or moral considerations? Organisations have unclear aims in common because they exist in an unclear world. This means that there are lessons for schools from looking at industry. Much modern management theory deals with uncertainty in aims and means as technology and markets change fast. This is relevant to schooling where goals are also unclear and changing, and where it is never easy to know how to achieve them. There are however important features of schools that are not shared with other organisations.

a   *Schools are passionate, political places*
Schools may seem boring places as they are reduced to routines in management training, but their importance at national and individual level is too easy to ignore. Politicians may have little evidence that standards in this country are better or worse than those elsewhere, but they rightly worry that economic wellbeing has something to do with the quality of schooling. Political concern with education has certainly increased since the mid-1970s among governments of both left and right. The succession of Education Acts in the 1980s is a feature of this concern.

Longer lasting, and for teachers more pressing, is the perennial concern of parents for the education of their children. Rich and poor alike justifiably see schools as important for future prospects. As with the national concern, teachers are in a difficult position. They are responsible for the schooling of groups of children. They cannot base their practice on anything as distant as the state of the national economy. Neither, however, can they easily adjust the education of the many to meet the demands of the parents of the few. That does nothing to lessen the passion with which parents will press for special considerations for their child, or groups of parents for their children.

Both national and individual concern are understandable. Schooling is important. There may be little evidence on how and why, but that does not diminish the passion. Schools may be placid places on the surface, but around them are the immediate hopes of concerned parents, the distant anxiety of politicians and the ever-present worries of children. All this concern is concentrated on what is learned. Teachers have to live with the consequent political pressure. All the evidence points to this involving more than responsibilities for academic performance. For example, teachers in primary schools give top priority to moral issues (Ashton, 1975). Their role is diffused, not contractual, unlimited in scope and hence exposed to emotional heat. Thus schools can be tense places in which to work. The passion is not often a problem in industry and is missed by outsiders writing about schools (see for example Everard, 1985).

b   *Teachers maintain a high level of independence*
It is important to stress the collegial nature of schools. Teachers do exercise responsibility as a group of colleagues, whether in agreement or not. But many organisations containing doctors, lawyers, financial experts, management consultants are also collegial in their operation. Yet it is possible for teachers to adopt a private role within their own classroom and to have little to do with colleagues in decision-making. This independence accounts for the extraordinary variety in the learning experiences of children in primary schools, despite LEA, HMI and DES recommendations (see Chapter 6 for examples).

Some nursery classes can be copying writing while in others the walls are regularly scrutinised to ensure that the children never see any words. This infant teacher assumes that children are not ready for addition and subtraction, but next door children the same age are being taught their sums. One teacher is shocked by the National Curriculum, the other welcomes it. Once the classroom door is shut there is autonomy. With rare exceptions teaching is a private affair.

At the heart of this privacy lies the nature of learning in schools. Because children are individual and because their learning is heavily influenced by the homes from which they come, teaching has to be flexible. This suburban teacher can lecture the class and expect them to respond positively. That inner city teacher has to organise so children can learn in very different ways given their different backgrounds and motivations. The free-wheeling professional in a government office or private corporation can be a nuisance. But in a school, each teacher adjusts to the children taught to give each a fair chance.

c *The distribution of information in schools is oddly bounded*
The importance of information is stressed throughout this book. This is partly because the 1988 Education Reform Act is so demanding. But it is also because the availability of information affects not just the distribution of authority within schools and between staff, governors and parents, but the organisation itself. 'Middle management' is tending to disappear in many organisations because information technology means that they are no longer necessary to collect, select and repackage information. This can be obtained by all from a computer. That is not a prospect in schools. But this discovery that much time is spent by managers in repackaging information is important. It suggests that schools and the education service in general are typical of traditional organisations in having top–down information flows. In Chapter 2 it is suggested that the 1988 Education Reform Act changes this to a circular flow more typical of modern organisations. The implications of this are spelled out in Chapter 9.

The possibilities for a teacher to perform effectively inside a classroom without engaging in discussions with colleagues point to the most important difference between schools and most other organisations. It is possible for learning to be organised in classrooms without the teacher responsible knowing or even caring much about how the school is managed. It isn't hard to find teachers who at the start of the year walk into a classroom of children already allocated to them, use the resources provided without negotiating for them, keep apart from the rest of the staff and know little of what is going on around them. In Chapter 2 it is argued that the 1988 Education Reform Act makes such teachers a menace. Nevertheless they will continue to work and often effectively. That points to why schools are unusual organisations.

This capacity of schools to survive with independent teachers who 'just do their job' suggests that schools have unusual information flows. Most organisations contain employees who do little beyond the job for which they are paid. All organisations control the way information is distributed. It is impossible for anyone in them to consider all that is available before coming to a decision. Life is too short for that. So there is incomplete or bounded rationality (Simon, 1945). In other words, individuals always make decisions with incomplete information. But in schools there is also the possibility of a divide between management information flowing down and professional information concerned with learning flowing up. We are near to the heart of the problem over the way learning gets out of management training.

The headteacher and senior staff of a school, after discussions with the governing body, will decide on the staff and other resources that are necessary for the organisation of learning in the forthcoming year. The decisions will be discussed at staff meetings and will determine the curriculum, staffing, support and resources for the teachers. The content and circulation is controlled from the top. In any organisation those at the top know what is going on because they get all the information while handing down only selected parts to those below. That is often why headteachers seem to be so knowledgeable. They are in the know. So they should be. They have all the information going across their desk. This gives them authority.

The teachers, however, remain responsible for the organisation of learning in their classroom. They may, as suggested, take no interest in why they have this many children or this sum of money to spend. Few teachers bother about costs. When local financial management was introduced into a Cambridgeshire primary school the headteacher asked staff for estimates of how much it cost to run the school per year. These ranged from £20,000 to £2,000,000 (Stenner, 1987). It was actually around £165,000. But teachers are responsible for learning and they control the information on learning which flows upwards. That remains the position even now that National Curriculum assessments have to be organised as part of school management. Headteachers need the information on what has been taught and what has been learned. But this is still to be based on teacher assessments across key stages. Much of that information will remain with teachers. They restrict it because there is too much of it to send up, because much of it is in a form that only they understand and because they too exercise power by restricting the information they release. They are doing just the same as senior management, for just the same reasons. The rationality of management decisions in schools is likely to remain bounded just where it is most important, because management information moving down is not necessarily related to information on learning that could move up.

Thus there is a schism in the information distributed in schools and this is reinforced by its role in sustaining both the authority of senior staff and professional autonomy. Management data is passed down selectively. Decisions in the classroom will hence be made with restricted rationality. But information is also being controlled by the teachers. The flow up of professional information on learning is similarly restricted. Information on management and on learning is controlled in different places and flows in separate channels, one down, the other up. Bringing them together is a hard task for a brave headteacher. But it is essential following the 1988 Education Reform Act.

There is a second problem in the distribution of information. Because learning is affected by factors in the home, it has always been necessary to give parents information. Yet that has rarely been organised. The problem arises partly from the time and energy involved. But once again it is related to the way information is intentionally restricted, not only to avoid confusing the recipients, but to retain professional control. All professions do this. The doctor even writes prescriptions so the patients can't understand them. Each profession has developed a professional language that flannels the customers. Parents have rarely received the information that would enable them to play a focused part in the education of their children.

The 1988 Education Reform Act builds on the 1986 Education (number 2) Act to secure a statement of curriculum aims in the prospectuses of schools and reporting of attainment to parents at ages 7, 11, 14 and 16. The intention is 'to give parents the information necessary to support as informed dialogue with the school' (DES, 1989b). Thus school management has now to take on board not just the collection and distribution of more information, but sharing it with parents. Further, information on the performance of the school on National Curriculum subjects will also be made public. The Act breaks the professional grip on the flow of information across what has in the past been a boundary between home and school that was carefully controlled by teachers.

d *Schools are uncomfortable at the leading edge of change*
Many organisations thrive only if they maintain a position near the leading edge of change. That applies particularly to the business firm in a rapidly changing world economy. Failure to innovate as markets change leads to disaster. This also applies to organisations such as hospitals where there is an advancing technology or the office faced with advances in computerisation. But schools do not face heavy pressure to adapt to changes in their markets or in the available technology. Indeed, conservatism often pays off. That is partly because the new technology often turns out to be inadequate, inappropriate, premature, or just plain daft. What happened to all those curriculum projects, programmed learning, teaching machines? Those who wait often do best. It is also because the learning that is valued is usually not immediately applicable to changes in vocational and other skills. Indeed, chasing computer studies, or integrated studies or French in the primary school can penalise the children that take these subjects. Conservatism among teachers often has just cause.

This caution about change in education does not mean that schools can be unresponsive to the demands made on them. Across the late 1970s and 1980s Education Acts forced teachers to give parents more information and to accept increases in the powers of governors. That responsiveness is the main objective of the education reforms at the end of the 1980s. Some steps had already been taken. Many primary schools in particular moved to accepting parents as partners in the learning of children. But the demands from parents are also often far away from the leading edge of change. They are as likely to demand Classical as Computer Studies. That is realistic as it is the minority, traditional subjects that have high prestige. The independent schools, responsive to their market to secure customers, have adjusted to the need for science, mathematics and technology. But they have also preserved a traditional approach to learning. This has enabled them to dominate the three-good-A-levels market, the entrance to Oxbridge and to high prestige engineering departments in other universities. Many maintained schools play this traditional game. The leading edge is safest observed, noted, but not chased pell-mell.

3 *The evidence that is available is often ignored*

Researchers have been attracted to schools because they have always spent ten or more years as pupils in them, find them on their doorstep and are welcomed by teachers. Thus the sociology of education has always been the most popular area of interest among members of the British Sociological Association and there are a lot of psychologists working in classrooms. Across the 1960s and 1970s, the study of the curriculum produced another host of researchers. More recently social scientists from many disciplines have investigated the factors behind school effectiveness. In each case the researchers find a ready audience in teacher education and can draw on international evidence. They can also draw on HMI evidence collected as part of surveys or published school inspections.

This is one of the richest collections of evidence on any organisation. Yet it is largely ignored by teachers and in school management training. Curiously, reflections on school management use as much evidence from studies of 'excellent' business firms as evidence on schools (see for example, Handy, 1984). These 'excellence' studies are described in Chapter 9. They depend on identifying the characteristics of successful firms and then on building up a composite picture of the excellent. It is the approach used by HMI and researchers on school effectiveness. This makes the neglect of the published evidence even more mystifying.

There is also the massive body of evidence on how children learn. This evidence is frequently the subject of INSET, particularly in popular courses on reading and special needs, but it is unused in management training. It is not easy to escape from the controversies in this evidence to solid ground on which teachers can build, but it is the theme of this book that learning should have priority. It seems lunatic to ignore a hundred years of psychological evidence, however much it is riven with dispute.

4 *Schools interact with rapidly changing environments*
This is the subject of Chapter 3. In the establishment of schooling
in the nineteenth century parents of the poor often objected to
the imposition of a demeaning and often patronising education
on their children. They objected to their children being stopped
from working and contributing to the family income. Schools
were imposed on an often unwilling populace. The move away
from this division between school and community has been slow.
But teachers are now faced with communities that are changing
fast not just in a material way but in their level of education.

The consequences of social change are rarely considered in
school management training. The variety in catchment areas is
hence under-estimated. Even in depressed inner city areas there
is wealth. This has come through raised incomes and particularly
through home ownership and capital appreciation. There is also
variety in the skills available out there, particularly as high tech
and service industries flourish. The unskilled working class has
been decimated in the last twenty years. Even more important,
there is now more cultural variety round the schools; there are
more children who speak two languages and more parents who
bring a different experience to bear than that being experienced
by their children. The danger in ignoring this change is that the
education given may be preparing for a world that is disappearing.
With a universally-educated population there is a prospect of
bridging the gap between education and schooling.

5 *Schools are involved in wide-ranging, radical changes in public
policy*
The final problem with books and courses on school management
is that they treat the education service as isolated from the public
services of which it forms a part. In particular, educational policy
is not related to wider policies changing the way welfare is allocated in general. The consequence is to miss developments that
are of immediate importance to staff in schools. This accounts for
the panic now visible as the 1988 Education Reform Act
is implemented. This mistake will be repeated unless school
management is placed in the context of further policy changes.
Schooling isn't separable from the health, housing, social security,
employment and personal social services. In the terms used by
Beveridge in planning the welfare state, the Evil Giant of Ignorance

could only be beaten as Idleness, Disease, Poverty and Squalor were conquered (Beveridge, 1942).

The emphasis on learning and on the provision of information on it in the Chapters that follow is partly to rectify its previous neglect in management training. It is partly to meet the priority imposed upon teachers in the 1988 Education Reform Act. The reluctance of teachers and of the academics responsible for their initial and in-service education to accept responsibility for attainment has been spelled out for over ten years (see for example Shipman, 1979). It is difficult to lay out the outcomes of schooling and the 'value added' by teachers. But in the end children and teachers suffer if it is claimed that it cannot be done. Governments are not generous to professionals who claim that their work has no measurable outcome. Thus the view that teachers were responsible for evaluating the processes of schooling but not the products and that the evaluation should be protected from public scrutiny had only a brief if happy honeymoon in academia.

The focus on learning, the acceptance of a responsibility for the progress of children, for the development of schools in changing environments cannot however be the responsibility of teachers only. The 1988 Education Reform Act gives parents as consumers extra information and the right to choose schools. But as consumers they have also to accept that they have a part to play. Schooling is a contract. Teachers should not be expected to labour with roomfuls of stroppy youngsters who stop others from working and smash up the school. School management has to inform parents of these duties and teachers have to support moves to bring responsibilities home to parents and children. That is part of the synoptic view of management that I recommend. There is an opportunity post-1988 to manage schools creatively. That is the implication of local management. It cannot be confined to staffroom and classroom. As parents become partners they have to accept responsibilities.

This book is about school management training as a means to improved learning. The 1988 Education Reform Act may be unwelcome, but it spells out both ends and means. It is an opportunity for remedying the neglect of learning, the paucity of information for decision-making and the consequent sterility of training that preceded it and is in danger of following it. If school management training continues unreformed, the 1988 Act will only create more stress and more confusion. There is now an opportunity to remove the boredom and at the same time make school management an opportunity for raising attainment. That aim is common to teachers, inspectors, administrators and politicians alike. It is also the hope of parents. It is the rationale for this book.

2 School management after the 1988 Education Reform Act

In Chapter 1 I argued that management training has failed to capture not only the learning and the information which supports it, but the enjoyment that lies at the heart of schooling. Schools are made to seem boring as well as aimless. Worse, the evidence for managing schools effectively has been ignored. Somehow managing schools has come to be seen as separate from the accumulating knowledge on how they work. Simultaneously, management training has lost sight of the ends for which schooling had been organised.

The danger in this situation persists as school management is geared to the new conditions post-1988. Indeed, while the priority given to INSET on school management has been increased, the approach to management training remains restricted. Yet the 1988 Education Reform Act was radical. This can be gauged by looking at any book on schooling published early in 1988. Thus *School Matters* (Mortimore, 1988) divides the factors in running a school into 'policies', over which the teachers have control, and 'givens' that they have to accept. The Act had the dramatic effect of changing the important 'policies' into 'givens' and vice versa. Thus the school curriculum and the involvement of parents were moved from 'policy' to 'given', while resources, intake and even status were moved from 'given' to 'policy'. Further, the Act contains two major yet conflicting themes. The intention behind open enrolment and local financial management is to give more scope for enterprise by shifting 'givens' to 'policies'. But the National Curriculum moves schools in the other direction by making it a 'given'. Enterprise and constraint have been introduced together.

The mixture of constraint imposed from the top and enterprise encouraged at the school level may have been contradictory, but it did bring opportunities for teachers to take more responsibility where it mattered, in the school, with the children. It is a time for those concerned with school management to lift their sights. Management has to be more than the introduction of routines. Routines will follow once the synoptic, strategic, creative aspects of management are in place.

This Chapter outlines this synopsis for a post-1988 management of schools. It keeps the attainments of children in the foreground. That is also a strength of the 1988 Education Reform Act. The Act reiterated the demands of the *Better Schools* policies (DES, 1985b) and of the HMI *The Curriculum from 5 to 16* documents (DES, 1985b) that policies must be aimed at raising standards for all. The focus on the end-product can be summarised in the word 'entitlement'. All children, of all ages, aptitudes and abilities are entitled to schooling geared to high standards. That is the task of management. It is also used as the justification for the National Curriculum.

The overlap between the major recommendations

The changes in the 1988 Act can be summarised for management purposes by looking at the way the Act has produced three new packages for school management; one for learning, one for resources, one for politics. These are illustrated in this diagram which indicates the overlap between them.

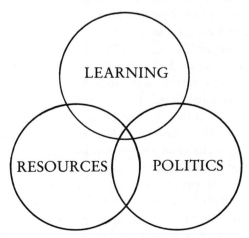

The three circles in the diagram each represent a package of measures introduced and tied together by the 1988 Education

Reform Act. The importance of this packaging lies partly in the content of each and partly in their overlapping. The content of each means that schools must now be managed with learning in mind. The overlap between them means that the achievement of that learning has to take account of costs and of the new powers granted to governors and parents. The links consist of information, made available to all parties and spelled out in the Act.

The three packages are not new in education. The 1988 Act consolidated them. They have been developed bottom-up by teachers and top-down by HMI and LEA over more than a decade. The legislation often went against the bottom-up developments. But it still left scope for them to continue. The view taken here is that it is a duty for teachers to continue their development of schooling by using the Act creatively. That is expected in the legislation which spells out what the Secretary of State cannot do. Examining the packages and their relation is a first step in continuing that bottom-up initiative and the accompanying search for valid and reliable evidence on the conditions which promote better schools.

The learning package

Following the 1902 Education Act, the Board of Education specified the content of both elementary and secondary school curricula in detail. Since then there have been periods such as the 1930s and 1960s when central government relaxed its control, and others such as the 1940s and 1980s when it tightened its grip. That is consistent with the role of central government in this country. It acts to restrict excessive local variations in the provision of services such as education. The evidence on the variety in the primary school curriculum in the 1970s is presented in Chapter 6. The curriculum of secondary schools ceased to be a problem for central government once the Secondary Schools Examination Council approved public examination syllabuses from 1920. When the curriculum development movement was started in the 1960s the very title 'Schools Council for Curriculum and Examinations' suggested that the lesson over the leverage of public examinations even in primary schools had been learned. Yet for over twenty years after the establishment of the Schools Council in 1964, curriculum development was pursued without radical change in public examination. The connection of curriculum and examination was largely ignored, even though the two branches of the Council shared a building and a title.

The key figure in bringing examinations and assessment into the van of curriculum change was Sir Keith Joseph. The Better Schools initiative in 1984 (DES, 1985b) explicitly related curriculum policy to the reform of examinations and assessment. Sir Keith was critical of the constraint of a national curriculum when proposals were discussed in the House of Lords. He wanted schools to have freedom to be different once they were in the market. But he had already pressed ahead to GCSE and closed the Schools Council. The Better Schools policy was largely about assessment and appraisal (DES, 1986). By the mid-1980s the assessment-led curriculum was clearly visible.

There is now a curriculum and assessment package. The national curriculum is spelled out by first defining attainment targets. These are then divided into ten levels, giving the steps up which children are expected to progress from 5 to 16. Reporting will be done at 7, 11, 14 and 16. In between these ages teachers will assess progress up the attainment targets. The reported levels will give confidential information on individual children to teachers and parents along with some data to enable parents to compare the performance of their child with those of peers in the school. Aggregated scores will be made public on the standards achieved in the schools at these ages. These will not be controlled for background factors but will be accompanied by descriptive data to put results into context.

The key point in this package is that learning is assessment-led. The attainment targets define the curriculum. Further, the information from the testing is supposed to guide teachers and parents as they help children. It is supposed to be formative. Assessment becomes the link between curriculum and learning. This has not been popular with teachers, particularly those of young children. Yet the formative use of assessment has always been supported by teachers and pressed by academia. It is the assessment used by all teachers as they help children learn. There is a threatening accountability aspect to this learning package with assessment at its centre and information on results released to parents in confidence on their own children and to the public on the performance of the school. There is doubt about the possibility of combining formative and summative assessment into a practicable yet reliable system. But it is no longer possible to treat curriculum, assessment and the attainment of children as separable. School management can no longer leave these matters to individual teachers. The 1988 Act makes them the responsibility of management by opening them to public scrutiny.

The resources package

From the early 1970s, the Inner London Education Authority allocated money to schools so that decisions about spending could be made by those who would benefit or suffer from them. More recently there were experiments to extend this local financial management. But in only two LEAs, Cambridgeshire and Solihull, working with volunteer schools, was the money allocated for staff salaries as well as other resources. Yet salaries accounted for up to three quarters of the running cost of schools.

The 1988 Education Reform Act tied together staff and the remaining costs in the school. From then on, decisions about curriculum, pedagogy, school organisation had to take account of costs. In particular, those decisions had to consider the cost implications of staffing developments. The Act produced a resources package that caused teachers to consider their own cost for the first time. Introduced with a principle of maximum delegation, this package is likely to affect all but the smallest schools. The package of financial delegation, formula funding, open enrolment, delegation of staffing to governors and performance indicators has justifiably been labelled a voucher system (Thomas, 1988). It puts schools into a potentially competitive market situation.

Once again, this is a cohesive package, which I have labelled 'resources'. Costs, whether in terms of money, staff time or energy have to be taken into account in school management. Opportunity costs have to be on the agenda. If teachers agree to do this they cannot spend the money required on something else. Further, while Local Financial Management increases the independence of teachers as they plan their curriculum, the DES requires LEAs to monitor financial delegation to schools. Schools through their governing bodies are accountable for their budget management. Schools will be expected to produce performance indicators (see for example Coopers and Lybrand, 1988 and

Statistical Information Services, 1988). Lists of the proposed indi-cators have been received by teachers with disbelief. They seem crude because it is so difficult to define ends and means in schooling. Again, this is a difficult situation for teachers. If meaningful perform-ance indicators cannot be produced it is difficult to defend spending on the education service. Yet the indicators are likely to produce distorted comparisons between schools. The amount of information will be increased here as in the learning package, but there is no guarantee that it will be reliable or valid.

The political package

The 1988 Act continued the movement across the 1980s towards giving increased powers to governors and to parents. It also introduced open enrolment. That gave parents the ultimate power to fill or empty a school. With resources tied to the number of children this altered the political balance dramatically. As long as the school had room it had to accept children, LEAs could no longer limit entry here in order to keep an unpopular school open there. The combination of open enrolment and local financial management was a gift of power to parents. If they removed their children, resources would drop and getting rid of teachers would be the only effective way of staying within budget.

The Act gives school governors influence over the hiring and firing of teachers, over the curriculum and over the budget of the school. Further, there is a campaign to recruit, train and inform governors of their new powers. It is unlikely that a distant relation-ship leaving headteachers free to act and then inform governors can persist (see for example, Adams, 1989). Once again it is the flow of information that will be critical. As this flow increases, governors will be able to increase their influence. Further, much of this will be on sensitive professional matters such as pupil performance, and through this, on the performance of teachers. The political package will open up areas previously protected by staff.

The Act also strengthened the powers of parents and governors directly. Parents were given rights to initiate proceedings for the school to opt out of LEA control and to receive more information on their child's and the school's performance. They had the right to appeal to the LEA if unhappy about the way the National Curriculum was being introduced. If they were still not satisfied they could appeal direct to the Secretary of State. This political package opened up the boundaries of schooling and brought external influences into the working of school management. The balance of power has been shifted away from the professionals.

The implications for school management

The diagram at the start of this Chapter has two important features for the management of schools. First, the packages overlap. Management of one is tied into the management of the others. Once again this is a new situation. If the curriculum is changed, the resources have to be found within the school, not from the LEA. The support of the governors has to be obtained and the wishes of parents must be considered. Similarly, changes starting in the resources package or the political package will necessitate changes elsewhere. Any management decision has to take the interaction between the packages into account.

The Act has integrated previously separable aspects of the school. That lesson has still to be learned. Books rushed out after the Education Reform Act in 1988 continue to recommend steps to local financial management or to the National Curriculum as if each could be separated. The Local Education Authority Project (LEAP), for example, first produced training packages on managing change, staff development, the curriculum, resources and accountability. These have little to do with learning or with the close relation between the different modules.

The second feature is that although the headteacher can still be seen at the centre where the three packages overlap, each package requires managing in new ways, and each involves *all* staff and consideration of other packages. Teachers are no longer insulated from political or financial decisions. As they organise their teaching, staff will be affecting the allocation of resources; and their actions will be of concern to parents and governors. At the same time the amount of information being produced and circulated will increase. The headteacher will not be able to cope with all these contingencies. Delegation becomes essential, yet insufficient. Being at the centre can still mean being overwhelmed. The only solution will be to empower staff to take decisions. Management has to involve the spread of leadership, not just delegation.

The three packages point to the necessity of a synoptic view of schooling, and hence to management through review of the whole school rather than of discrete parts. With that broad view the implications of the 1988 Act can be sorted out. That isn't easy because there are tensions in the Act between the rhetoric of the market and the reality of accountability, between an emphasis on enterprise and compliance with a National Curriculum. The constraint is not supposed to reduce enterprise. The Act is supposed to provide a framework for the National Curriculum within, across and beyond which teachers are expected to produce a distinctive schooling. Just as the National Curriculum Council is charged to ensure that the balance across the curriculum nationally is not distorted by the claims of individual working parties recommending excessive programmes for core and foundation subjects, so teachers retain the responsibility to ensure that their school retains the balanced and broad curriculum that is the entitlement of all children.

The new or changed factors now facing school managers are listed below. They have been flagged over the 1980s, particularly in the policy statement *Better Schools* (DES, 1985b). They are also visible in initiatives started in schools and in LEAs. That is no surprise. The 1988 Act was one of a number of measures taken to move the public services into the market, where demand is sovereign. It was based on policies developed over more than a decade since the education service came under political scrutiny in the early 1970s. Many of its features had already been introduced locally because they met new demands arising from population changes, which are described in Chapter 3.

1 *From loose to tight structure*
The emphasis in HMI and DES publications in the 1980s was on securing 'greater clarity about the objectives and content of the curriculum' (DES, 1986). It was also about improved examination and assessment, about the effectiveness of teachers and about more power for parents, employers and others outside the education service who were seen as influences for a more vocationally relevant schooling. The 1988 Act confirmed this trend, not just in spelling out a National Curriculum through the specification of Attainment Targets, but in spelling out the conditions for more tightly monitored schooling. Ends were defined through

targets and means specified to meet them. Across the 1980s the pre- and in-service education of teachers was given similar treatment through the specification of criteria that restricted the scope for higher education to decide the structure of courses.

This tightening of the structure of schooling conflicts with the emphasis on increased power to parents as consumers. In a market, producers aim for a differentiated product. Further, there is no evidence that coupling ends and means closely together leads to better schools. Certainly effective schools know where they are going and their staff know the part they should play. But effectiveness also comes from the school culture, from leadership in all its variety, from colleagues meeting and talking together. Tightly coupling ends and means may constrain some wayward staff, but can stifle the very enterprise that the Act is supposed to encourage. Managing by pottering around is not just effective in high-tech industry. The combination of a warm culture and a clear structure remains the best safeguard against sterility in schooling.

2 *From administration to management*

When LEAs held the purse, fixed the intake numbers for schools and appointed teachers, it was possible for schools to be administered without much thought for the morrow. The financial, demographic and staffing decisions were made in County or Town Hall. Even more important, planning was done for the schools. The 1988 Act and particularly the local management of schools, pushed accounting, budgeting, staffing and forward planning down into the school. Simultaneously it gave greater powers to governors to influence these decisions. The routine application of procedures laid down from the LEA is no longer sufficient. School management now has to include costing, planning and monitoring. It needs more information, much of it from classroom teachers.

The most important change is, however, the assumption in the Act that schools will not only meet statutory requirements, but clarify their objectives and teaching methods and help parents to contribute to raising attainment. This is an invitation to adopt an active, entrepreneurial management style. It suggests that there should be a vision not just detail. The National Curriculum is a constraint, but it is attached to a package that frees staff to plan their own way forward. That invitation for management to be visionary as well as efficient aligns schools with modern organisations faced with rapidly changing markets. It is why management theory is relevant. This point is taken up in Chapter 10.

3 *From authoritarian to collegial responsibility*

As the need to manage increases, so there is pressure to spread the responsibilities for management in the schools. That is the implication of the overlapping packages outlined at the start of this Chapter. All staff are now making decisions that will affect management. All staff have to be involved and aware of this new situation. As the structure is tightened, so the professional, collegial contributions of staff have to be incorporated into its management. Professional organisations such as schools allow freedom within rules that are often unwritten but accepted as necessary. Now many of those rules, including responsibilities and directed time, are being written out as means are coupled more tightly to ends. Each teacher is inevitably involved. Management has to be shared, securing conditions for each teacher to be an effective influence.

This is the consequence of the overlap between the three packages outlined above. Few schools may have organised to use collegiality effectively, but its importance is clear (see for example Bell, 1988). As the century closes collaboration as a team will become even more vital. Local management assumes that all teachers will be involved and cooperative. The weight of work will have to be shared. Since 1987 teachers are supposed to have specified responsibilities as part of the regulations on their pay and conditions. With local management all will have to carry responsibilities. The most important come from the increased power given to parents and governors. Unless teachers act as a team, unless all pull together, the image of the school will be tarnished. Reputation is the basis for marketing schools. They have to be visibly effective.

The spread of responsibilities makes the problem of the uncoop-erative teacher even more pressing. That is why teacher appraisal has continued as a priority when it could have been left to the combination of open enrolment and Local Financial Management which would result in unpopular schools having to shed staff. One uncooperative teacher can now hold back the release of information that is mandatory. That teacher can negate any attempts to market the school. The 1988 Act assumes a staff that pull together.

4 *From economic insulation to opportunity costs*
It has not been necessary for teachers to be aware of the costs of
schooling. Costs were never the concern of initial or in-service
education. This insulation from costs can be seen in lights left on
and windows open with central heating going full blast. But it is
most noticeable where it matters most. With around three-quarters
of costs going to pay staff, the financial implications of both
existing and proposed curriculum and organisation are rarely
understood. That is not confined to teachers. In all the evaluations
of curriculum projects launched by the Schools Council there is
no mention of cost. It is ignored in the academic literature. Yet
it is the major concern of DES and LEAs as they contribute to
the annual Public Expenditure Survey Committee and haggle over
who gets what. Local Financial Management brings opportunity
costs into the school. If money is spent here it cannot be used
there. The budget cannot be left to the local authority treasurer.
It has to be the central part of planning the curriculum, staffing
and organisation of each school.

5 *From producer-power to consumer-power*
The coincidence of Local Financial Management and open
enrolment with the increased powers to governors and parents
has shifted power to the consumers of schooling away from the
teachers. That has been intentional and in line with moves in
local government, public service and nationalised industry. It
means that teachers can no longer insist that they have the right
to determine the curriculum and the extent to which parents can
be involved. This is a major change in English education.
Elementary schooling tended to be imposed on an unwilling
populace in the 19th century. Up to 1988 teachers still tended to
restrict parents to marginal activities and to exclude them from
influence over what was taught and how. The 1988 Act spelled
out the rights of parents to information about their children and
gave them remedies if they were not satisfied that the National
Curriculum was being implemented.

This shift in influence partly resulting from open enrolment
means that schools are now having to take marketing seriously.
Customers have to be attracted. Competition is likely to hot up.
This is justifiably distasteful to teachers as it has been to lawyers,
doctors, opticians and direct labour forces faced with competition.

But that is the intention. Parents are expected to exert influence. Teachers are expected to respond. There is no mystery about why this has happened. Since 1979 the Conservative government has been limiting the rights of professionals, as of the rest of organised labour, in order to increase competition. In education it is intended to produce the choice for the poor that has previously been the preserve of the rich.

6 *From top-down to circulating information*

Through all the changes listed above thread demands for more and new information. That is a major challenge to school management. The close relation between the three packages will also alter both the quantity and direction of information flows in schools. The 1988 Act demands more information, not only on the assessment of children, but on the performance of the school as a whole. Much of that has to be provided by teachers. It has to be made available to governors and parents as well as LEAs. The separation of management from academic information described in Chapter 1 has to be bridged. Not only assessment data and performance indicators but records of achievement will give more information to the public. The demand for financial and accounting information is also increasing. This follows from both the planning and accounting in Local Financial Management. Teachers have to plan their predicted expenditure, management has to decide on the budget and allocate it. Governors have to approve and play a part in accounting. Part of the accounting goes beyond figures to judgements about benefits from spending. It will be increasingly difficult to control information on grounds of professional autonomy.

There are two striking aspects of this change in the production and circulation of information. First, it puts pressure on teachers. Much of the data required from them is now mandatory. It is tied to management information. It has to be reliable. For example, National Curriculum assessments are supposed to be aligned with Standard Assessment Tasks and externally moderated. Information is essential to management and it has to go on the agenda as a priority for management training. The problem is that the demand for information has built up so fast that few examples of good practice exist. It is too early to look to information technology for much relief. It can help in recording, storing and retrieval. But the use of comment banks and grades that can be easily computerised has not been welcomed in records of achievement, either among teachers or among employers and other users (DES, 1989a).

The second aspect is that information passed down from head-teacher will now have to be synchronised with that demanded from teachers. Further, much of that information will be distributed to governors, parents, LEA and DES. It will be the link between the learning, resources and political packages. That re-direction of information will affect the organisation of schools, particularly the structure of authority. This is discussed in Chapters 8 and 9.

Continuing developments in the schools

In addition to changes introduced from outside, teachers develop their own curriculum and teaching methods. That isn't expected to cease with the National Curriculum. Indeed, the 1988 Act prescribes the powers of the Secretary of State and assumes that schools will compete on the basis of their distinctive organisation. Many of the developments are longer-term and only slowly affect the school. That is an advantage. It gives time for the weaknesses to be detected and eliminated. Thus as a school staff consider the way forward in the 1990s they will need to be sure that they do not erase the bottom-up developments that give their school its strength.

The list of teacher-driven innovations that follow can be detected in many schools. Many of these developments are now incorporated into public examinations such as GCSE, CPVE and BTEC. Many share the principles of progression, criterion-refer-encing and formative assessment recommended by the Task Group on Assessment and Testing in 1987 and accepted by the Secretary of State for the assessment of the National Curriculum (DES, 1988). Yet the list is often overlooked in school management. Indeed, because the management information is often not infor-med by that available from teachers on learning, the developments are sometimes not known to exist.

1 *Developments in what counts as valid knowledge*
This is a continuous development, largely the result of accumulated

changes introduced by teachers. It can be seen in the stress laid by HMI on knowledge, concepts, skills and attitudes as the elements of learning (DES, 1985a). That is now the language of education. It would have seemed strange fifty years ago. The emphasis on skills in particular has increased in both primary and secondary schools. Below this new emphasis is another profound change in the priority to school learning. Learning outside the classroom and school is being acknowleged as valuable within school assessment. This is partly a recognition that personal and social skills are crucial to academic learning yet are affected by external factors. It is even more a realisation that extra-curricular learning is valuable in itself, and should be recorded and encouraged. That is why records of achievement are given the task of assessing 'across and beyond' the national curriculum and include extra-curricular activities.

2 *Developments in improving the effectiveness of learning*

The evidence on the importance of reinforcement is reported in Chapter 7. It has been absorbed into teaching. The terminal examination at the end of a year or school career clearly does not provide useful feedback for learner or teacher. Hence the rapid growth of modular courses which break up learning into digestible parts yielding frequent results for guidance. These courses are popular because they often ease the organisational problems of time-tabling. They also encourage learners. Graded assessment was the fastest growing area of public examination in the early 1980s for the same reason. The learner and teachers get frequent information. In the primary schools curriculum materials, guide-lines and checkpoints similarly contain built-in guidance.

3 *Developments in assessing what has been learned*

The dependence of teachers and learners on rapid feedback (which is stressed in Chapter 7) has encouraged moves to build formative assessment into courses. Many curriculum materials contain such exercises, guiding pupils by regular assessment which can point to remedial or extension work. But there is a more profound change in the basis of assessment as teachers move from norm- to criterion-referencing. There has always been criterion-referencing and it is easy to over-estimate the differences between using norms and criteria as references. Payment by results in the 1860s for example was based on simple criterion-referenced tasks for children. The real change is the realisation that a grade or mark without reference to what has been learned yields very little information and can be misleading. Referencing against norms gives some comparative information. It is useful for selection. But only when it is against objectives or criteria does assessment yield information that can be used to identify strengths and weaknesses as the first step to remedial action.

4 *Developments in allocating responsibilities for learning*
This development is the least advanced yet the most exciting. The 1988 Act spells out new rights for parents and governors. It limits the rights of teachers, particularly over the curriculum. In this new balance the professionals have diminished power. Parents need no longer accept a place in a school because there is no alternative. They can, in theory, shop around. If they don't like the curriculum in the school they can query it. They have a right to evidence on how well their child is doing in relation to others at age 7, 11, 14 and 16. They will receive information on standards in the school in comparison with those elsewhere. But in a market, rights go with responsibilities.

There are moves to confirm the legal responsibilities of teachers (see for example, DES, 1989d). There are also moves to establish those of parents (see for example DES, 1989c). Consumers have responsibilities. 'Let the buyer beware' is a warning that the producers have limited liability. The conditions laid down in contracts on the purchase of goods or services often have legal status. If you misuse the goods you can't claim your money back. This reciprocity has yet to come in education, although government has started to spell out the rights of schools to claim money from parents, in cases such as examinations entered but not sat. The 1988 Act increases consumers' rights, but does not spell out duties. That is a task for the future. It is also a task for the teachers.

The 1988 Act also redistributes responsibilities between teachers and pupils, across schooling from 5 to 16. Learners do best when they know what they are supposed to be doing and can take responsibility. Such a redistribution is a necessary component of individualised learning. It is an attempt to give children and their parents a say over targets for learning and behaviour. It is visible in the formative assessment and negotiation in records of achievement. The redistribution of responsibility is also built into the establishment of compacts, wherein employers contract to give preference to pupils who fulfil terms of achievement and behaviour laid down for the last years of statutory schooling. The Inner London Education Authority, for example, pioneered the London Compact to bind pupils to specified levels of behaviour in exchange for priority in obtaining employment with the firms in the scheme.

All these developments are detectable in legislation and in projects sponsored by examination boards and LEAs. But they have their momentum among teachers in schools. They are genuinely bottom-up. They have to be taken into account when the 1988 Education Reform Act is being implemented because they are the hope for the future as well as what gives schools their distinctive flavour. There are three reasons for hoping that these developments will flourish. First, they are in line with principles accepted for the implementation of the Act. Second, teachers will fight very hard to preserve them; they are valuable for their children in their school. Third, they are a response to social changes that will not stop in 1988, but will accelerate into the future.

3 Social change and social policy

School management has been transformed by the 1988 Education Reform Act. But that Act was itself the end product of a long line of measures taken to change the education service. Further, the policies behind those measures were themselves responses to rapid changes in the economy and in the structure of the population. These responses have altered direction dramatically in the 1980s. The origins of this shift can be traced back at least twenty years. School management is forced to respond to social change, whether indirectly through legislation or as a direct response to changes in the lives of children and their parents. This Chapter looks first at the evidence on those changes and then at the policy changes behind them.

Much of the evidence presented is from the Government Statistical Service and published annually in the HMSO publication *Social Trends* and from the Office of Population Censuses and Surveys (OPCS, 1988). It can seen to be dry facts. But behind these lie the lives of parents struggling to do the best for their children. The statistical picture also understates the wide variations between regions, areas, classes and individuals. Teachers face very different social conditions in the catchment areas of their schools. For each comfortable, academic institution in a leafy suburb there is another facing the deprivation of a run-down inner city. For each teacher able to relax with well-motivated children, there is another doing the dirty work that we would often prefer to pretend does not exist. Some schools face a hostile or indifferent external environment and have difficulty avoiding chaos inside. School management here will not suit there. Books and courses inevitably over-generalise. The reader should look beyond the statistics in this chapter to the varied reality behind them.

Changes around schooling

1 *Population structure*

- We are getting older as a population. The odds a hundred years ago were against living to 54. Today the odds are that men will live to 71, women to 77. In the UK, there are now 700 thousand people over the age of 85. This will double by 2025 to 1.4 million. By then there will be more people over 70 than children in primary schools.
- The number of live births in the UK was 1,015,000 in 1964. It fell to 657,000 in 1977. That fall is still working its way through schools. Primary rolls are rising slightly while secondary rolls are still falling. There were 755,000 births in 1986. The number of births projected for 2001 is 759,000. The prospect is for school rolls to stabilise around the mid-1990s.
- The number of births per head of all British women fell between 1971 and 1986, including women living here, but born in Asia and the West Indies. The number of births per woman in the 20 to 24 age group fell across this period largely because women delayed having children.
- Immigration under the Immigration Act of 1971 fell from 82,400 to 46,800 between 1975 and 1986. Citizens from the New Commonwealth and Pakistan made up under half this number.

2 *Family Life*

- Only 10 per cent of families in the Census of 1981 consisted of two parents and two children with father at work and mother at home.
- Britain has the highest rate of divorce of any European Community country at 13.2 per thousand. Denmark was next highest with 10. The rate in Britain was 2.1 in 1961. Divorce affected 152,000 children in 1980. In 1987, 32 per cent of children of divorced couples were under five. In 1972 this was 23 per cent.
- Between 1971 and 1987, births to unmarried mothers increased from 8 to 23 per cent of all births, despite improved

contraception. There were 61,000 births to unmarried mothers in 1976, 158,000 in 1986.

- 14 per cent of all dependent children live in one-parent families compared with 8 per cent in 1972.

3 *Economic activity*

- The total labour force rose from 24.9 million in 1971 to 26.7 in 1986. At the same time the percentage of women working in the age group 25 to 44 rose from 52 to 69.
- Unemployment rose from 4.3 per cent in 1979 to 11.5 per cent in 1986. It then fell to under 10 per cent in 1988 although the basis for the statistics also changed.
- The number working in manufacturing has fallen from 8.0 million in 1971 to 5.2 million in 1986. The number working in services has risen from 11.6 million to 14.5 million between those years.

4 *Income and wealth*

- Taking 1980 as 100, personal disposable income was 77 in 1970 and 117 in 1986.
- From 1976 to 1986, the 20 per cent with the highest disposable income increased their share of the total from 38 to 41 per cent, while those in the lowest 20 per cent received a decreased share, even though their actual incomes still rose.
- Top rate tax has been reduced from 83 to 40 per cent and basic rate tax from 33 to 25 per cent between 1970 and 1989.
- In 1988 there is 60 per cent home ownership. Between 1961 and 1986 the number owning houses increased from 7 to 14 million. From 1980 to 1986 one million council tenants bought their houses.
- Houses have rapidly risen in value. In the South-East grandmothers will be leaving houses worth over £100,000 to their children. Many of these will be over 40 and own their own houses. There will be an increasing number of moderately rich people. It has been calculated that by the year 2000, £9,000,000,000 will be passed down each year in this way (Economist, 9/4/88).

5 *Regional differences*

- The Northern region has the highest unemployment in 1987 at 14–15 per cent. The South-East had the lowest at 7–8 per cent.
- East Anglia has the fastest growing population of any region at a rate of 5.1 per cent between 1981 and 1986. In the same period the Northern region lost 1.2 per cent of its population.
- The highest qualifications in the workforce are in the South-East where 13 per cent are graduates. 5 per cent are graduates in the Northern region.
- The highest expenditure per head on supplementary benefits in 1981–86 was in the North-West region.

6 *Social class differences*

- Researchers have continued to find gross material differences between the social classes (see for example Mortimore and Blackstone, 1981). Children of unskilled workers have higher mortality rates, a lower birth weight, more illness, worse teeth and will report more symptoms of ill-health throughout their lives.
- The inequalities of social class affect education. The children of unskilled workers are twice as likely to need special education than the average. On average they will under-attain at every age in all subjects (see for example, Burgess, 1986).
- 6 per cent of children attend independent schools. But 28 per cent in universities are from these schools, rising to 48 per cent in Oxford and Cambridge.
- There is considerable social mobility, much of it achieved through educational qualification. Most of this takes place in and out of the middle class. The most hereditary, immobile group is the unskilled working class. Their children do not tend to rise up the social scale (Halsey, 1978).

7 *Sex differences*

- From 1970 to date, female wages as a percentage of male wages rose from 55 to nearly 70 per cent, but the move to equality has slowed down.
- In 1971–2, 18 per cent of the members of the British Medical Association were women. In 1980 this had risen to 22 per cent.

- Girls attain higher than boys in the first years of schooling. At 'O'-level more girls than boys take French and biology, but fewer take mathematics and physics. At 'A'-level this difference widens and the number of girls reading mathematics and the hard sciences in higher education is small.
- 6 per cent of girls and nearly 9 per cent of boys are reading degree courses.

8 *Ethnic differences*

- In 1984–86, 17 per cent of Asian and 21 per cent of West Indian males were unemployed compared with a national average of 10 per cent.
- In inner London, 20 per cent of all families had only one parent in 1981. The figure for West Indians was 43 per cent, for Asians, 5 per cent (Keysel, 1982).
- West Indian children do as well as other children at entry to infant schools (Tizard, 1988). But West Indian boys then slip behind further as they are tested at successive ages (see for example ILEA, 1983). They achieve fewer 'O' level passes at higher grades than either their Asian or White peers.

These statistics give a crude picture of life in contemporary Britain and of current changes. Behind them lie wide variations between regions and within them. Neighbouring schools may receive children with very different material backgrounds and very different levels of motivation. The fastest changing conditions are for young women who are less worn out by childbirth, are better educated and more likely to be employed.

It is not just the introduction of more power to school governors and to parents, or of local financial management and open enrolment that makes it essential to manage schools in the light of knowledge about the local communities. All the evidence points to the importance of social background in influencing attainment within school (see for example, Burgess, 1986). Teachers have always adjusted to different home circumstances among children. But these efforts in the classroom may not be reflected in school management training. The environment of schools is also neglected. Yet the evidence is overwhelming that schools are effective while they work with parents or have their support. That means knowing the environment in order to manage an effective school. This outgoing focus of management is no easy option. Out there parents are doing a lot of educating. They have formed a lot of voluntary groups. They belong to pressure groups that may seem hostile to teachers. The evidence on that communal activity is important if school management is to be informed.

Communal activity

On average men watch over 25 hours and women watch over 30 hours of television per week. There is a wide social class difference. Those in the top two classes watch 20 hours on average while those in the lowest two classes watch 35 hours. They are also likely to be watching different programmes. This may give the impression that there is a dormant population around schools, particularly in working class areas. Attendance at parents evenings may confirm this. Yet a search around even the most deprived community will turn up an active concern with self-help, with helping others, with getting things done, with ear-bending and pressure grouping. It is difficult to reduce this to a statistic. From 1975 to 1985 the income of charities doubled to £12,700,000,000. A lot of that came from the poor. A lot went to helping children.

It is also easy to ignore the growing educational and technical qualification of the population. Secondary schooling for all was introduced in 1946 and its effects should have been felt. 74 per cent of the age group 25–29 in Britain hold at least a CSE qualification compared with 42 per cent in the group aged 50 to 59. Between 1975 and 1986 the percentage leaving school with at least one GCE pass at A, B or C grade 'O'-level rose from 49 to 53 per cent for men and 53 to 59 per cent for women.

1 *Voluntary activity*
In one deprived area of Birmingham are youth groups, groups for the disabled, senior citizens groups, church groups, special needs groups, carnival committees, youth clubs, young mothers groups, Scouts, Guides, Cubs, Beavers, Brownies, Woodcraft Folk, Covenanters, Air Training Corps, Army cadets and Naval cadets, community arts groups, community centres, family centres, friendly societies and cooperatives. Many people belong to many of these. Few belong to none. Many groups actively seek out the

lonely and the deprived. They have organised a housing repairs cooperative, installed litter bins, protect telephone booths and keep the estate tidy. These are active community members making life tolerable for themselves and helping others.

This communal activity is not confined to any particular ethnic or religious group. Many of these organisations span such groups. In this area of Birmingham there are Sikhs, Moslems and Hindus, Rastafarians and Christians. The Black churches and the Moslems are particularly active. These and other groups have developed networks throughout the area. They know who can advise, who can help, who needs advice, who needs help. They educate their young, support the old and help the deprived.

All these groups liaise with social services. Many receive money from the local authority or through Inner City Partnership or some other funding to alleviate deprivation. Social workers depend on them for information and support. There are often professionals among them excited by the opportunity to be in direct contact with those who can use their skills, whether as artists, actors, musicians, teachers or social workers.

2 *Education in the community*

It is trite to say that not all education takes place in school. It is important to stress that a lot of schooling takes place in the community. Let us return to our estate in Birmingham. Here are Mothers and Children groups, Playschemes, Kids groups, Playgroups, Nursery groups, After School Clubs, Children's sessions, Mencap, sports training groups and clubs where mothers can learn how to help their children at school. Once again there are often professionals involved. But there are many more volunteers, learning as well as helping.

Among the ethnic minorities the activities became more actively educational. There are supplementary and Saturday schools among the West Indian community. These are trying to make up for what is seen as an inadequate maintained schooling. There are schools among Asian groups ensuring that the children grow up knowing their own culture, religion and language. There are schools primarily concerned with Sikh, or Bengali, or Gujerati or Rastafarian culture. But they are also educating as the children read, listen, recite and calculate.

It is easy to see the reason for all this voluntary educational activity when the diversity of many inner city populations is considered. A survey published in 1981 the Inner London Education Authority reported that there were 131 different languages spoken in their schools (Inner London Education Authority, 1983). In other towns there may not be as great a variety, but there will always be groups determined to preserve their culture among the young. The education in the community helps the schools. Often there are connections made and the voluntary groups can help teachers with children who have a difficulty with language. But the variety is also a rich cultural feature. Many of the children will grow up able to speak two languages. It is a remarkable facility common to rich and poor alike, under-utilised in schools.

3 *Pressure groups*

From the Society for the Protection of the Unborn Child to the Society of Embalmers there are pressure groups from cradle to grave. They generate the energy of political action locally and nationally. They range from multinational corporations trying to influence central government over foreign policy to two or three parents seeking to get a lady to cross children to a school. It is often undemocratic, who you know rather than how representative your case, but pressure groups cannot be ignored. As the powers of school governors and the rights of parents are increased, so will the activity of these groups around schools.

There is a particularly rich crop of pressure groups concerned with the family and education. The Child Poverty Action Group dates back to the rediscovery of poverty at the end of the 1960s. MIND, the National Council for the Unmarried Mother and her Child, and Gingerbread are other well-known examples. There are others such as Family Forum which coordinate the activities of many groups. Similarly there are numerous groups pressing for educational change or against it. The more formalised have been labelled the 'sub-government of education'. The churches are the most influential. There are the local government associations and the teacher unions and professional associations such as the National Association for the Teaching of English. There is the National Confederation of Parent–Teacher Associations which federates the Home and Schools Council, the Parent-Staff Association and the Friends of the Schools. From there on, there is a mass of acronyms such as CASE, ACE, CREEM, CAUSE, PRISE and FEVER. There are left- and right-wing groups. The Pre-School Playgroups Association grew to become a major provider of places for young children from the efforts of a few volunteer mothers.

From inside the school this proliferation is often confusing. It is difficult to know which groups are representative. This is particularly difficult in forming a governing body. Many of the groups have a short life. Others are subject to successful takeover bids. Many a headteacher has consulted an organisation, thinking that it represented an ethnic group only to find that next week it is an outcast. It is not uncommon to be subject to simultaneous pressure from one group wanting to abolish and another to pre-serve corporal punishment or school uniform or skirts for girls. Yet such groups are a sign that parents and others are not passive. There is intense political activity around schools, just as there is a lot of voluntary work and a lot of teaching.

It would be absurd to ignore this wealth of educational and supportive activity when looking at school management. It is a remarkable feature of the history of schooling in this country, particularly for the poor, that it has often been imposed on an unwilling population rather than being built with them. Large-scale historical studies and small-scale case studies show a reluctant and often resentful working population resisting the spread of schooling on offer (see for example, Hurt, 1979 and McCann, 1977). Schooling has often been seen as patronising as well as removing the wages of children from the family. Parents have only recently been welcomed in primary schools and there is still a professional resistance to using parents to help educate their children, despite the evidence on the value of cooperation (see for example Topping and Wolfendale, 1985).

Using the network of voluntary associations around schools is high-risk activity. But the description above was of an area where the schools have difficulty and where school management cannot be exclusive. The children in primary as well as secondary schools bring their experiences from their community into the classrooms. Their capacity to learn is affected by their life in family, street, club and church. Managing schools with an eye on learning means accepting the power of this education outside school and working with it.

The political response to social change

To understand what has happened in the education service, and
hence to uncover the new context for school management, it is
necessary to look at social and economic change. New social
policies have been introduced across all the social services, and
the direction of economic activity, particularly in relation to local
authorities and nationalised industries, has been changed (see for
example Shipman, 1984). Up to 1988, most writers on education
looked forward to a return to the days of consensus. They failed
to notice that the whole approach to social policy had been
changed. Only with a longer view of the attack on the welfare
state can the current position of schools be understood.

It can be argued that the task of teachers is to oppose this
change in social policy. Most books and articles on education
took this view up to late 1988 (see for example Holt, 1988). But
the 1988 Act has made this a high-risk activity. Any school that
does not implement the National Curriculum or the national test
programme, or refuses to implement local financial management
will face two sanctions, even if the staff have the support of their
governors. First, the LEA will have to take action to secure
compliance with the Act in order to fulfil its statutory obligations.
The local inspectorate have that task as a top priority. Second,
with open enrolment, parents are likely to remove their children
to schools that are following the National Curriculum and getting
respectable scores on the accompanying assessments.

It is important to trace how the education service has been
swept into a position where unpalatable medicines are having to be
swallowed. Only with that understanding can school management
organise internal affairs effectively and appreciate what is happening educationally in the communities outside. We may not like
the move from welfare to opportunity state. But children still
have to be educated. The look back for the reasons shows that
the days of consensus, of the welfare state twenty years after its
establishment, were still rife with injustice and inequality. The
1960s were no golden era for the poor, for girls, for the newly-
arrived ethnic minorities. Indeed, these issues, now face up on
the table, were then concealed. It is sometimes rewarding to cut

through the romanticism to the hard reality of the political change that produced alternative solutions for social welfare.

Social welfare at the end of the 1960s

The Beveridge Report of 1942 and the legislation, including the Education Act of 1944, that followed, established the welfare state by the late 1940s. Twenty years later evidence had accumulated that it wasn't working. That evidence was not confined to education. There was a 'rediscovery of poverty'. The documentation of persisting poverty came in a book significantly titled *The Poor and the Poorest* (Abel-Smith and Townsend, 1965). This book documented the persistence of poverty, particularly in the inner cities. It placed particular stress on the poverty in families with young children. The Child Poverty Action Group was one response to the shock of this evidence. The findings were confirmed at the end of the decade with the dramatically titled *Poverty, The Forgotten Englishman* (Coates and Silburn, 1970).

After 1965 the evidence accumulated that something was wrong with the social services (Edwards and Batley, 1978). The inner cities received particular attention and the Community Development Projects at the end of the decade were followed by General Improvement Areas, the Housing Action Areas and so on up to the Inner City Partnerships of the 1980s. Section II of the Local Government Act 1966 was used to help the immigrants from the New Commonwealth. There was also concern over housing, where the Milner Holland Report of 1965 spelled out problems; and over social services where the Seebowm Report recommended major changes in 1969. Beveridge's 'Evil Giants' were still with us.

The evidence on the impact of education flooded in across the 1960s. The studies of Douglas, particularly *The Home and the School* (Douglas, 1964), showed that gross inequalities in schooling had continued. The poor were still getting a rough deal. This was confirmed in the Plowden Report (DES, 1967). But most comprehensive was a summary of the available evidence titled *Born and Bred Unequal* (Taylor and Ayres, 1969). This laid out a factual position of the disadvantages faced by the poor across the country. By the end of the 1960s it was clear that working class children were losing out within the welfare state and had not improved their relative advantage within education despite secondary education for all.

This accumulation of evidence on failings within the welfare state was met by a flurry of measures for improvement. The personal social services were reorganised. Money was made available for improving the inner cities. There was an effort to find and help the poor. But the solutions threatened the principles underlying the welfare state itself. The difficulty in remedying problems came from the assumptions in the legislation in the late 1940s that it formed a comprehensive system of social services. The basic principle used by Lord Beveridge, incorporated into the legislation that provided the social services including education, was universalism. The services were to be paid for by all and used by all. There was to be a national health service, a comprehensive system of social security covering needs from cradle to grave. There was to be education for all. Underpinning the social services there was to be full employment. This principle of universalism was of course never satisfied. There had always been private medicine, private insurance, private schooling. The action to remedy the problems emerging in the 1960s was based on positive discrimination. Now special groups were to be identified for special help. Universalism had not worked. It was a rallying cry in wartime. It incorporated beliefs in a united nation. It became increasingly difficult to maintain as peace brought special rather than universal interests to the fore.

Education was typical among the social servics in switching to positive discrimination at the end of the 1960s. The Plowden Report recommended Educational Priority Areas and these were organised as action research projects around 1970. Even more important, LEAs switched funding to helping schools in poor areas. The Inner London Education Authority for example resourced its schools on a combination of children on roll and measured deprivation (Shipman and Cole, 1975). Schools in deprived areas were given extra staff and special allowances. Many received teachers funded under Section II of the Local Government Act of 1966. The search was on for ways of boosting the chances of the children of the poor following the evidence on their continuing low achievement. The principle of universalism was broken to help specific groups.

In retrospect the attempt to discriminate in favour of the poor and later on behalf of black children and of girls in education was over-optimistic. The resources were always small. The personnel involved were few. The adverse factors were massive. Furthermore, the effort to pinpoint schools in need of extra resources soon led to complaints that those who were successful were being penalised, while those teachers who got poor results were being rewarded (Shipman, 1980). Even before the decade was over the first attack from the right of politics had been launched at education in the form of a Black Paper (Cox and Dyson, 1969). It was the first sign of a radical shift in policies for tackling social problems.

The replacement of the welfare state

Faced with the evidence that poverty and inequality had survived the welfare state, politicians first diverted small sums of money to the large tasks identified. Those policies persisted to the 1980s. In education they can be traced from the educational priority areas programme at the start of the 1970s to the Lower Achieving Pupils Programme at the end of the 1980s. By then the momentum behind positive discrimination had gone. The initiative had passed to those who wanted competition not compensation, enterprise not dependency, provision through the market not by the state, power with consumers not producers.

The left of British politics accepted the universalism that was at the base of the welfare state. The solution for them was to provide more resources to improve the public services. But this was difficult at a time when the problems remained and the economy was in poor shape. As early as 1969, Richard Crossman was telling the Fabian Society that the social services could not forever meet the demands being made on them (Crossman, 1969). He was in a good position to know. He was the minister responsible for Social Security.

The right-wing evidence is rarely among the references in books. Yet it has captured the intellectual initiative as well as the ear of government. The Black Papers at the end of the 1960s were the first public indication that a new force was emerging in education. Long before then the Institute of Economic Affairs had been researching and publishing on public attitudes to the social services. These surveys suggested that the public was disenchanted with the welfare state and was not willing to start paying for more welfare (see for example Harris and Seldon, 1979). The Institute of Economic Affairs was established in 1957. It was the first of a new brand of right-wing think tanks that have thought up the basis of the opportunity state into which schools have now been thrust. Later, the Centre for Social Policy, the Social Affairs Unit, The Adam Smith Institute, the Freedom Association, as well as the Bow and Hillgate groups came up with a simple if brutal alternative to the welfare state. The apparatus had to be demolished wherever possible and services returned to competition. The capture of the public services by professionals had to be reversed.

The privatisation of the nationalised industries is a parallel move. Another is the insistence that hospitals and local authorities use competitive tendering for the services they require. Most important here is the insistence that the population must cease depending on the state for services and must take personal responsibility wherever possible. Welfare was to be distributed through the market.

Underlying all these recommendations for replacing the welfare with the opportunity state was an attempt to provide a stronger economic base. The Beveridge Report and the thinking behind the welfare state does assume that full employment was possible and that workers would cooperate to enable the wealth to be created to support universal welfare. This turned out to be optimistic. The Labour Party lost the 1979 election after rubbish and dustbins littered the streets and the dead weren't being buried. But that winter of discontent was only one act of a long-running failure to get the economy moving. With the International Monetary Fund called in in the early 1970s to keep the economy going, the chances of plugging the gaps in the welfare state were slight. From 1979, the Conservative government has tried to limit public spending while streamlining the economy. Prominent among the economic policies was the reduction in the power of the trade unions which were seen as frustrating attempts to make British industry and services more competitive. By the end of the 1980s the white collar and professional associations were also being weakened.

From dependency culture to enterprise culture

The current central government policy in education is part of an attempt to shift the country from a dependency or benefit culture to an enterprise culture. It is a simple idea. The welfare state is seen as encouraging the belief that personal initiative, even hard work is not necessary as the state will, in the end, provide. Why should those who save for their old age pay for others to draw supplementary benefit? Why should the feckless be protected from their own lack of effort? Why should not those who struggle hard for their children see the results of their labour instead of watching the state compensate others who haven't tried? Why, to give an example from Digby Anderson, the director of the Social Affairs Unit, should a child be able to attend school from 5 to 16 making life a misery for other children and for teachers and then leave without any qualifications and expect to draw supplementary benefit that will be paid for by those who did try hard (Anderson, 1987)?

We will never know whether the benefit culture did produce dependency and reduce initiative. We do know that voters seemed to think that a change was needed in 1979 and across the 1980s. In that time much of the welfare state has been demolished and competition has been inserted even into the health service. We are now expected to buy services that were previously free, to train for work or not receive benefit, to receive loans rather than grants and to buy housing rather than rent it from the council.

From corporatism to the market

The 1960s were the decade of big planning, big government, an enlarged civil service and local government. It was the era of the quango, the quasi-autonomous government organisation of which the Schools Council, established in 1964, is an example. It was the decade of indicative planning and the Department of Economic Affairs. In education it was the period of the huge early comprehensive schools. It was the period when social scientists predicted the establishment of the corporate state. As industrial disputes were settled over beer and sandwiches at 10 Downing Street between Prime Minister, CBI and TUC, workers could be excused for thinking that they were not being consulted. As trade unions negotiated with government to fix the annual pay rise, the individual was left little scope for enterprise. Nationalised industries received increasingly large subsidies. Prices were fixed by marketing boards, while retail price maintenance took care of the shoppers.

The education service expanded with the rest of the public services, particularly as school rolls went up in the late 1960s. The teacher unions were at their strongest. Early in the decade Sir Ronald Gould, the General Secretary of the National Union of Teachers was strong enough to stop the Minister of Education from discussing the school curriculum in the Ministry (Manzer, 1970). That was the business of teachers not politicians. The professionals had established their position. Teacher education had expanded and the move to a completely professionally-trained teaching force was given legal status. Above all, those in education, like the remaining public services, assumed that expansion would continue. In 1974, *Education: A Framework for Expansion* was published. Mrs. Thatcher was then Secretary of State for Education. Ironically it ushered in the years of contraction.

The sudden ending of the threat or promise of corporatism has been remarkable. It has been accelerated by contraction in the education service as elsewhere. Once school rolls fell, the bargaining position of teachers evaporated. The government has now abolished even the Burnham Committee that negotiated the annual pay award. It no longer bothers to appoint teacher union representatives to working parties and committees which, a decade ago, were dominated by them. Today you sit by Sainsburys rather than the National Union of Teachers when discussing curriculum or records of achievement or testing. Professional matters are decided without consulting the profession.

The day of the consumer and the market has arrived. The producers can no longer dictate the terms. Books and articles may still reflect the cosy days of consensus and the liberal left or extreme left in academia, but the real power to determine policy has gone to the right. By the end of the 1980s the Labour Party had set up the Institute for Policy Research to produce its own long-term strategy. But it has to be remembered that the right-wing think tanks laboured for more than a decade before their views became political reality.

The implications for school management

The mix of constraint and opportunity in the reforms in the late 1980s provides the context for school management training in the 1990s. The weaknesses in that training point to the importance of taking the opportunities rather than bowing down under the constraints. Teachers will do this because their efforts to help their children in their schools require National Curriculum and assessment to be met alongside their own attempts to maximise learning. That is expected in the 1988 Education Reform Act. Schools are expected to determine how the National Curriculum is to be taught, and national testing is supposed to fit into assessment procedures already in place. The specification of core and foundation subjects is constraining, but even here, it is assumed that teachers will still produce a distinctive, tailor-made curriculum that is broad and balanced.

Thus initiatives are still expected. That is the way teachers will exercise local financial management, meet the wishes of parents and continue to develop education where it matters, with the children. If the century is to end with the enterprise culture and with schools in the market along with other public services, school management will have to be less constraining and more outgoing. The initiatives of teachers are not only in line with these developments, but are the guarantee that schooling will provide a suitable environment for learning as the world outside changes. If there is a sudden change in the direction of the political attack on the 'Evil Giants', nothing will be lost. Indeed teachers will have continued to perform their essential role of adapting schooling to ensure that conditions for learning remain stable, effective and fair.

Thus it is possible to end this review of policy on an optimistic note. The 1988 Act was supposed to usher in a period of enterprise, despite the constraint of the National Curriculum on the variety of schooling that could be put into the market. There is also another reason for optimism. Social and economic change is probably accelerating, not slowing down. This will create new demands on teachers. They will have to continue to develop the schools bottom-up to ensure that the conditions for effective learning are not redundant. The world did not stop in 1988.

4 The school in the service: decision-making in education

Education is a service full of idealists, forever frustrated. The combination of rapid social change and radical legislation has already complicated the lives of teachers. The legislation has to take precedence, but the social changes will continue to produce new demands. School management will have to be active, not just in putting the learning, resources and political packages described in Chapter 2 into place, but in further developing schools to meet the trends described in Chapter 3. It cannot be assumed that the necessary decisions will be straightforward and rational either inside schools, in county or town halls, or in central government. The more aggressively any one party acts, the more frustrated the rest become. Decision-making needs to be scrutinised.

Frustration is often due to impotence
The official descriptions of the education service as a 'national system, locally administered' or a 'partnership' of central and local government and the teachers, indicate the spread of power. The service is often described as 'distributed', 'disseminated' or 'decentralised'. Again, the indication is that the levers for change are spread among different agencies. Legislation doesn't guarantee anything will happen inside the classroom. The grip of central government has been increased across the 1980s. Pupils, parents and employers have been given more say. The management of schools has now to respond. But there is still a rich soil for the unexpected and unintended.

Frustration can be found at all levels. Ministers of Education don't stay long in post. Legally they direct the service. In practice they have found other hands on the levers that get things changed. David Eccles found that he was not supposed even to discuss the curriculum. Fred Mulley complained that the nearest he was supposed to get to what went on in classrooms was over the removal of air-raid shelters, hopefully redundant, after the second world war. From her subsequent behaviour, Margaret Thatcher does not seem to have enjoyed her time at the DES and Shirley Williams, then a Labour minister, initiated the Great Debate over standards and accountability in 1977. Politicians chairing Education Committees in local authorities were similarly advised that the curriculum was to be left to the teachers. Their advisors, the Chief Education Officers, have also been vocal in complaining that they have no real power and that the days of great CEOs are over. By the end of the 1980s many were retiring early. Curiously, ministers and DES officials, local politicians and CEOs all complain that they can't find the levers of power. But the same complaint was loud and clear among teacher unions in the 1980s. In the education service the levers of power always seem to be held by someone else.

Headteachers also buckle under increasing administration, the flood of memos to be answered, the questionnaires to be completed, the need to account, to inform, to consult, that leave little time to act as a leader of a group of professionals. Teachers are also complaining. They also feel that they have lost responsibilities for the curriculum, are pressed by administrtaive burdens and are not adequately appreciated or rewarded. Teaching is never the placid transmission of knowledge to eager children. There is discipline to maintain, there are materials to get ready, there are individuals who need special attention. The teacher's day is punctuated by interruptions. Having eyes in the back of your head wears you out.

All this frustration is added to by legislation increasing the part played in schooling by governors and parents. This affects teachers as they help children and advise parents. The head is increasingly involved with school governors over what is taught and how. Since 1974, LEAs have become intensely political. The service is peppered with pressure groups, supporting or opposing aspects from comprehensive schooling to smoking among teachers. Schools are supposed to be responsive to parents, to employers, to further and higher education. As the Secretary of State is pressed at Question Time in the House of Commons, so this parent is asking a teacher for special treatment for a child and employers are complaining that applicants lack essential basic skills. Below the frustration lies intense political concern about education, frequently grounded in personal interests.

Administration is easier than management

It is easier to administer education than to manage it. It is also less frustrating. The two are easy to confuse. In central and local government, and in schools, there are responsibilities to provide enough places of the right kind for children to be educated. That is a major concern. Getting the right people into the right place at the right time takes a lot of effort. The DES takes responsibility for the school building programme, the closure or change of use of schools and the training of teachers. The LEAs ensure that the children are in schools that are adequately resourced. The teachers organise the timetable to ensure that these children receive the National Curriculum. From DES to school classroom, established routines ensure that the Secretary of State for Education fulfils 'the duty . . . to secure the effective execution by the local authorities under his control and direction, of the national policy for providing a varied and comprehensive educational service in every area' (Education Act 1944, Section 1).

This routine administration takes up a lot of the time at all levels of the service. Indeed two reports on the English education service in the 1970s concluded that policy seemed to be confined to ensuring that there were roofs over the heads of the children (Organization for Economic Cooperation and Development, 1975; House of Commons Expenditure Committee, 1976). The same emphasis could be found in LEAs and in schools. Priority is given to keeping things running smoothly. However, problems arise because the world around education doesn't stay still. Furthermore, a smooth running education service can still contain gross inequalities and injustices. It may be difficult to spell out aims for education and to find ways of achieving them, but that does not relieve those responsible for managing affairs from the duty to adjust to change, review practices and plan for improvements. Management is more than administration, more than keeping the lid on. Ensuring stability to ensure appropriate conditions for learning means change.

Things rarely work out as planned

A common element in the frustration that is voiced within education, in expansive as well as contracting times, is that the best-laid schemes usually go awry. People who make decisions in education live with the often unintended consequences of their actions. A teacher organises a break from routine and the pupils respond, not with delight, but with resentment. A headteacher decides that the use of the cane should cease, only to find that more use is being made of the slipper. Comprehensive schooling is introduced and the result is the reproduction of selection within each school. The Assessment of Performance Unit starts out in 1975 to monitor national standards over time; by 1985 it hasn't produced the expected time-series, has given up the technique chosen to do this, but is productively busy advising on the curriculum, the one area which it promised to avoid a decade earlier.

Decision-makers watch as their intentions are adapted by administrators and professionals to fit into the complexities of the service. Frustration at the top is often a symptom of adaptation lower down. This is frequently necessary to ensure that policies do not harm children. But in DES and county or town hall, it is still uncomfortable to live with the unforeseen and often unwelcome consequences of your decisions. Further, while the top decision-makers see their intentions being distorted, they notice schooling changing from the bottom up as half a million teachers take their own initiatives. Implementation is diffused through over 20,000 schools by over 400,000 teachers. The consequences are often not those planned.

Thus schools are the despair of the tidy-minded. The attempts to introduce MBO or PPBS failed at national, LEA and school level. The tidy-minded did not give up. The search for performance indicators goes on, encouraged by the yearning for accountability. But it isn't easy to account systematically for the 'spiritual, moral, cultural, mental and physical'. There is never enough reliable information. Consequently, efforts to produce performance indicators frequently look ludicrous (see for examples, Coopers and Lybrand, 1988 and Statistical Information Services, 1988). Accountability implies rationality, the implementation of intentions. In education, what is happening is often unintended and often undetected by those who have accounting responsibilities.

The frequency of unintended consequences in schools can be seen in the many studies of the hidden curriculum of schooling. Here the unplanned and often unintended consequences of grouping large numbers of children together in confined spaces, with timed routines, regular assessment, strict discipline and unequal relations with a few adults have been shown to produce unintended social and moral learning (see for example, Jackson, 1968). This has little to do with National Curriculum or LEA advice and all to do with surviving in the close quarters of a school classroom.

Unanticipated consequences can appear over time or with startling rapidity. Thus the 1988 Education Reform Act lays down aims for the curriculum and means through which it is to be organised. But that will not be the end of unintended consequences. Their most enjoyable feature is their unpredictability. The Key Stage 1 research teams got to work in January 1989, designing standard assessment tasks for the end of infant schools. Within a month they realised that, by assuming that five- to seven-year-olds were taught in an integrated, clustered, topic-based way that should therefore be assessed by cross-curricular tasks, they were about to convert a sizeable minority of infant teachers from their subject-based teaching. An Act intended to consolidate traditional subject virtues turned out to be having the reverse effect within a few weeks of the work on the ground starting.

These unintended aspects of schooling are frustrating for management, but a cause for optimism. Schools are never boring for those who study them. The unpredicted is a source of delight or despair. So it is for those who work in them. It may frustrate those who prefer neat hierarchies and clear lines of responsibility. But each school serves a different environment with different children and different teachers. There has to be adjustment to top-down legislation and advice. Teachers are experts in this domestication. They do it to help their pupils. As they do their best in their classrooms for their children, they often frustrate policies. But they also start trends that prove unstoppable because they are so beneficial.

Once again it is wise not to exaggerate the differences between schools and other organisations in the extent to which plans are frustrated in their implementation. The 'Yes Minister' syndrome is common in government and public service. It is not unknown in the private sector. Indeed, the recent change in management models for industry from rational, top-down and strategic to social psychological, bottom-up and cultural is confirmation that what's good for General Motors is often ignored among work-forces in Detroit and Luton.

Decisions are usually taken in ignorance

This sounds insulting to Secretaries of State as well as teachers. But it is not anyone's fault. At the heart of schooling lies learning. Over a hundred years of psychology have failed to give us more than the few solid pieces of evidence reported in Chapter 7. When decision-makers ask experts, inspectors, researchers, academics about an issue they tend to get a two-handed response. 'On the one hand it's like this, on the other hands it's like that'. While I served in London's County Hall, my Education Officer, Eric Briault pleaded for one-armed researchers. He never got one. Education is complex and so are answers to educational questions.

The problem is at its most frustrating where even descriptive data turn out to be unavailable. We don't know how many children are about to enter schools at five in an LEA. We know how many are born, but then we lose sight of them. Many parents will have moved, sensibly before the children start schooling. We may want to help raise the attainment of children of the unskilled working class, or children of West Indian origin, or children who move school frequently, but there are no figures. These are relatively simple statistics, yet it is both technically and politically difficult to obtain them. The Assessment of Performance Unit was supposed to assess the incidence of under-attainment. It never did so because there was no information that could allow the job to be done. Most intentions are frustrated in this way. In the end we make decisions on the best evidence that we have. Frequently that is personal experience, political belief or guesswork.

There is an important political conclusion sometimes drawn from this evidence. If decisions are made in ignorance, then making them at the top is liable to cause the most damage to the service. The safest way is to decentralise decision-making to schools. There the consequences of mistakes are felt directly. Their impact is localised. Direction can be changed quickly. Small is beautiful because you make your own mistakes.

The implications for school management

The difficulty in finding the levers to get things done in education affects the management of schools as it does that of LEAs and the national service. There are rarely any precise aims or adequate means to meet them. Furthermore, means are not closely related to ends. Information doesn't flow easily from DES through LEA to headteachers and on to teachers, as well as out to parents and employers. The flow of information bottom-up is a trickle. Similarly information across the service between teachers in the same school or different schools, between headteachers or CEOs or local politicians is limited. Loose-coupling of ends and means leads to insulation and even isolation.

It is easy to visualise this situation by remembering that there are three main levels of activity in the education service, central and local government and the schools. Within each there are political and administrative interests, and professional personnel. Management has to take account of these nine possible interactions all taking place without adequate information.

	Politicians	Administrators	Professionals
DES	Ministers	Civil servants	HMI
LEA	Councillors	CEO and AEOs	Inspectors/ Advisors
School	Governors	Headteacher	Teachers

Any management decision in government or school is affected by consideration of the nine possible interactions in this diagram. Once implementation is considered, pupils, parents and others have to be added.

Suppose a Chief Education Officer decides that each school in the LEA should have an assessment system, linked to the LEA, ready for the full implementation of Natural Curriculum testing. Discussions will first involve the LEA inspectors and Assistant

Education Officers. Once a scheme looks feasible it will be discussed with the Chair of Schools Sub-Committee or Education Committee. Simultaneously discussions will be held with headteachers and possibly representatives of teacher unions. The scheme will be aligned to legislation and phone calls will be made to Schools Branch in the DES. The HMI responsible for the LEA may be consulted. Before the proposals get to schools, local politicians on the Education Committee will have informed their colleagues on the governing bodies of schools. Political positions will be taken. The headteacher discusses the proposal with his staff, meets local inspectors, and explains it to the governors. Parents are informed. The teachers get advice from their union representatives.

That is the formal, surface interaction. Below it telephones are ringing and pressure groups are active. Teachers are fitting the proposals into their ongoing procedures. There are multiple interactions before the management of such a scheme can be attempted. Even then, most parents, many governors, some teachers and a few heads will claim that they have never heard of it long after others have implemented it.

Thus there are no straightforward lines of command in education. The usual response is to legislate and hope for the best. But the consequence has been a lot of frustrated effort. If resources are offered to schools they will take the money and use it for the general good. Even if LEAs follow the innovation up, the interest will soon flag. The history of curriculum development is not so much of tissue rejection, but of non-implementation. Most projects were accepted for the resources they brought. Schools then accommodated them into their ongoing curriculum. If the projects were based in higher education, LEAs even encouraged this domestication (see Shipman, 1974). When the DES allocates money from Educational Support Grants (ESG) for Lower Achieving Pupils, or Teacher Appraisal, or Records of Achievement, schools spend it in ways that promise long-term benefit. If MSC fund TVEI lavishly, schools take the money and reform the curriculum beyond its technical and vocational aspects. These are not dishonest actions. They are motivated by a desire to benefit children in the long as well as short term. For the best of motives, educational management has to live with unpredicted outcomes.

The political model of decision-making in education

The complexity of interacting interests is the normal context for management at all levels of the education service. It is the basis for understanding the management of schools. It is the daily insight of senior staff as they organise the school day, run their departments and teach. Getting things done means convincing professional colleagues. But it also means meeting the legal requirements, watching the pennies, aligning to LEA and DES advice and keeping a wary eye on the formal political views of governors and the informal politics of the staffroom.

In this interaction within the service each party, whether DES, LEA, heads, teachers, parents, pressure groups and so on put their view as powerfully as possible and press hard to get things moving their way. It is less partnership than partisanship. At the heart of this model is conflict not consensus. Indeed, if one party fails to push hard, the others get suspicious. Teacher unions are at their most alert when government seems to be agreeing with them without getting something in exchange. Insomnia among CEOs increases when politicians who are usually critical begin to smile on proposed developments. Headteachers get uneasy when staff receive proposals without demur.

It is easy to illustrate this interaction at national level. The history of the Schools Council shows how an apparently professional issue of curriculum development was settled only after many meetings to balance the different interests of the various partners in the service (Manzer, 1970). An apparently professional issue of the school curriculum was settled through political chicanery at meetings in the DES, in London clubs, union headquarters, county and town halls. Inevitably, given the involvement of diverse political as well as administrative and professional interests, the Council worked in ways that were unpredicted by those who established it. When it was finally polished off it was doing its work in ways that were not the subject of the political acrimony that marked its birth. The education service is organised so that goals are frequently displaced, initial intentions buried and new priorities adopted. This is conflict not consensus.

Models of decision-making

The unintended consequences of educational reform, the many interactions in a loose-coupled service and the potential of teachers to control the information on learning and subvert policies all counsel caution in modelling educational decision-making as rational. The part played by reason will be limited. It is essential for school management to be based on some model of the way decisions are formulated and implemented. Two models at least have to be considered.

Rational models
It is usually assumed that decisions are made on rational grounds and that these decisions are built into policies in a linear fashion. The version assumed in most books and courses on management is as follows.

This model is linear and rational. It assumes that issues are identifiable and that there is sufficient information to formulate and choose the best policies. The policy-makers, be they politicans with their administrators and inspectors, or headteachers with their staff, get together and sketch out possible ways forward. They collect together evidence to help decide between possibilities. That evidence is sometimes collected through systematic evaluation, although that is rare. Most decisions are made after considering only the experience or impressions of those party to the decisions. A few are made out of total ignorance. Only one thing is sure. There is never enough information, even after that rarity in the history of research, a thorough evaluation, delivered on time.

Once the decision is made, this model assumes the implementation is straightforward. But this stage has already been discussed as a minefield of unintended consequences. This is an over-simplified model, but it is useful. It focuses attention on specifying goals and ways of achieving them. It is often found, bent into a circle, in a systems model. It is the model used by the National Development Centre for School Management Training (McMahon and Bolam, 1987) to develop management tools such as GRIDS (Guidelines for Review and Internal Development in Schools). Unfortunately the model ignores political reality. Policies are rarely formulated rationally nor implemented in linear fashion. We need to look at another model for management.

A political model

Most educational policies are built up over time, often a decade or more. Further, they are implemented over a similarly long period. That means that they are usually overtaken by other developments. At any one time several, often competing policies, are being accommodated by teachers. Further, policies in education are not isolated from other social policies. Headteachers usually inherit policies as well as staff. The latter are often wedded to the former. Others want the school to go in the direction they favour. The way forward has to be political, to satisfy conflicting views in the best possible way.

FORMATION ◂▸ DECISION ◂▸ IMPLEMENTATION

In this model policies are formed over a long period. In the early stages this formation may be bottom-up, hatched in 20,000 schools. Later, it begins to be noticed and tidied up in town and county halls. Then the DES gets involved. The policy is formed incrementally. There is no point at which a reasoned decision after consideration of evidence starts the policy-making. This point may follow a generation of prior developments. The actual decision, legislation, memorandum may be the most dramatic event, but it takes little time and codifies what has already happened. There follows another long period of implementation. This is when teachers and others get to work on the policy and adapt, domesticate and subvert it. As they do so they are forming the next wave of policies for the next decades. This is neither rational nor linear. It is political and incremental. Above all it is unpredictable.

This model fits even the 1988 Education Reform Act as described in Chapter 2. The twenty years to 1987 were the formative years for right-wing educational policies designed to put education and the other social services into the market. The period

from the Consultative Paper of July 1987 to the 1988 Education
Reform Bill was the brief decision period. Implementation will
follow over the next decades. But grassroots, teacher-initiatd
developments will not cease. Implementation will still be unpredictable. That may be frustrating for policy-makers, but it is
also a cause for optimism regardless of political persuasion. The
bottom-up activity is a sign that teachers still take their job
seriously and are in touch with pupils and parents. It means that
they are fighting their corner of the service, where it matters,
where learning takes place. School management must never inhibit
that initiative.

It is possible to list the practical importance of the differences
in these models by asking questions that are of crucial importance
to the management of schools. These questions owe a lot to the
work of Weiss (1982).

Q Are the issues clearly distinguishable?
A The rational model of decision-making assumes that the
problem or issue can be defined, isolated for consideration,
distinguished from related concerns, treated as contemporary. In
practice, it is rare to find an educational issue that is not bound
up with other educational or social issues over a long period of
time. In Chapter 5 the close relation between social background
and achievement is discussed. As schools debate records of
achievement, or testing at 7, 11, 14 and 16 they relate the effects
to race, to class, to sex, to ability, to motivation, to the home
life of children and to the moral concern to help them all, not
just the fortunate. The rational model of decision-making implies
that issues have clear boundaries. The political model implies that
education is meshed into wider social considerations.

Q Is it possible to separate means and ends?
A Here we are at the heart of the difference between the two
models of decision-making. The rational model assumes that ends
can be distinguished and means worked out to achieve them. The
political model may acknowledge this ideal but assumes that ends
and means tend to get mixed up. We may know where we want
to go but rarely know how to get there. Projects such as the DES-
funded Lower Achieving Pupils or Records of Achievement pilot

studies, or MSC-funded TVEI, provide schools with money in advance of any clear definition of what is supposed to be done with it. That is the nature of development projects. One popular move in these three projects was to buy micro-computers assuming that they would soon become useful. Unfortunately the software often made this a false hope. Here the means were waiting for the ends to arrive. This is the reverse of rational. The linear move from issue to solution is reversed. Nor is this reversal confined to development projects. In the expansive 1960s and early 1970s many schools purchased tape recorders, video machines, programmed learning machines, computer time-tabling schemes, machines to teach reading and film cameras and then waited for someone to tell them for what purpose they could be used. Many ended up with the stuffed owls in the cupboard of discarded aids.

Q Is it possible to specify costs?
A The most frequently expressed caution about proposed changes in education is their cost. If teachers are asked to record, negotiate with individual pupils, increase the amount of continuous assessment, testing and homework marking, something has to give. Any proposal will be met by opposition based on a claim that it is disturbing priorities. This situation has been made more acute by the attempt to introduce some rationality into teachers' pay and conditions through regulations (DES, 1987). These laid down the days and hours of directed time. The consequence has been to make teachers aware of any extra demands on their additional hours presumed to be necessary to discharge their professional duties. These opportunity costs cannot be easily isolated because teaching is never confined to the purely contractual. Of course, the implementation of the 1987 regulations is also unpredictable. Many staffs seemed to have ignored the prescriptions or treated them so flexibly that change has been minimised.

These questions confirm that adopting a rational view of decision-making in education, and hence of school management, will produce hunches about the way things will work out that may mislead. It is necessary to accept that schools are complex social organisations and that teachers' subjective interpretations of what is going on can defeat the best-laid plans. It is necessary to take a long-term view, to consider how things got to the present state and how the school is working at present. It is necessary to accept that getting things done involves giving as well as taking, offering incentives to persuade people to change. It means consideration of the wider social context of the decisions to be made. Above all, it means accepting that rational decisions taken without consideration of the complexities of schooling can delay rather than promote much-needed change. That conclusion suggests that sometimes it is more effective to encourage initiatives among teachers than push them in a direction determined for them. It always means that the developments over time, in the classroom, around the school and by the teachers, with the pupils and parents, have to be respected.

The conclusion has to be that the political model of decision-making is the more valid reflection of reality. But that does not mean that a rational model has to be abandoned. That model has the virtue of trying to sort out ends and means. The translation of that rationality into practice depends in schools on bringing legal, administrative and financial information together with information on learning. That is important throughout education. It is the justification in the 1988 Education Reform Act for spelling out the information on attainments that must be given to parents and made public. Rationality in decision-making is a goal achieved when there is sufficient information.

Chapters 1 to 4 have outlined the weaknesses in school management and looked at the models that lie behind decision-making. The stress has been on the political influences at all levels of the service. I have ended optimistically. Education isn't a service where teachers can be buttoned down to ensure linear implementation of top-down decisions. That protects children from policies that assume uniformity in teaching. It allows teachers to plan for individual differences, for the varied backgrounds of their children, for changes in the environment of schooling. It allows enterprise where the learning takes place, in the classroom. The message for school management is clear. It must promote, not inhibit that enterprise. That is as true after as before 1988.

5 The evidence: school- and teacher-effectiveness

The management of schools is a national priority for in-service training. Its major weakness is that it has not been explicitly related to raising attainment. The research and inspection that have produced the relevant evidence have been neglected. The availability of HMI reports on schools (summarised in the *Education Observed* series), their surveys of primary, middle and secondary schools (published from 1978 on) and their publications on good schools (see DES, 1977b) and on good practice (see for example DES, 1986) have provided sources based on expert observation. Academia has provided studies of the effectiveness of secondary and increasingly of primary schools. These range from case studies (see for example, Armstrong, 1980 for primary and Burgess, 1983 for secondary) through large scale statistical studies (see for example Mortimore *et al*, 1988 for primary and Rutter, 1979 for secondary), to massive international collaborations such as the *International School Improvement Project* (OECD, 1986). There are also studies of teacher effectiveness (see for example, Bennett, 1976) and more general research on the experience of learners, ranging from nursery and infant (see for example Tizard, 1988 and Bennett, 1984) to secondary schools (see for example, Woods, 1980).

This evidence has been the focus of strong criticism. It is often contradictory. But it remains the most substantial source on the factors that make up an effective school and its neglect in many management books and courses is extraordinary. Once the hatchets are rested, one important finding remains. Schools can be effective. They can work even in adverse conditions. The research has uncovered the factors that mark these effective schools. Those factors should be central to the management of schools.

The strength of the research evidence arises from its exposure to criticism. The mark of good research is that it is published with sufficient detail to enable experts to criticise it. That ensures that the weak is distinguished from the strong. The weakness of personal experience is that it is not open to this scrutiny. It is private, not public knowledge. That does not mean that the research evidence is either completely credible or immediately applicable. Anyone taking a summary of the evidence as a guideline for managing a school would be in for some unpleasant consequences. Yet even the weakness of the research are useful in defining the limitations of the management of schools. The measures of effectiveness used have been the attainments and behaviours of children. These are often crude measurements. But they are more valid as indicators of effective schooling than the more general assumption that if a school is working smoothly, all is well.

The assumptions in the evidence

HMI and researchers surveying schools share a managerial view of schooling. That means it is based on a particular view of schooling as a means to an end. School effectiveness is defined in terms of achievement. That assumes that schools are a means to attainments that can be defined by the measures that are available to inspectors or researchers. There is an alternative view that schools should be pleasant places in themselves, that education is an end in itself and that human development is not reducible to attainments on tests or to observed behaviour. Indeed it can be legitimately argued that schools, particularly for young children, should not be expected to mould them through a National Curriculum, but should allow them, within a framework provided by the teacher, to grow naturally. Many teachers were trained to believe this and the Plowden report (DES, 1967) supported this developmental view. But it is a harder world as the century ends.

The second set of assumptions in most of the evidence is professional. Up to the 1988 Education Reform Act, it was usually assumed in books and on courses that inadequacies in schooling were best rectified by improving teacher education, by in-service training, by management courses, by teacher appraisal. These measures assumed that schools would be best improved by concentrating on professional practices. The 1988 Education Reform Act however cuts through this assumption by putting schools into the market through open enrolment. Now an effective school will expand and the inadequate will lose pupils. Hence they will gain or lose resources including teachers. If the improvement doesn't come, the school will finally have to close. The conclusions, even of studies of school effectiveness, have been overtaken by events. Even a book published in 1988 such as *School Matters* (Mortimore *et al*, 1988) concludes that parents must work with schools to produce gradual improvement rather than seeking another school for their children. The view taken is that of the professionals.

The implicit models

The managerial assumptions behind research evidence and inspectors' reports contain a set of implicit models of the school. Early reports contained simple models which have been steadily sophisticated. But all share the view of a school as a user of resources, human and material, to produce attainments. Here is a simplified view of the sequence through which this model has been elaborated in research. Even the simple output model without reference to the processes in the schools is still in use. Even the final and most sophisticated model is a simplification compared to real schools. As models they are best used as a source of hunches about the way schools work. Reality is more complex.

The output model

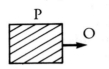

This is *ex post facto*, after-the-event research. There is no way of knowing what caused the outputs in the school.

The process-output model

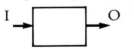

Now the outputs can be related to different school processes. But differences among intakes and their environment could still be major influences.

The input-output model

I → [ ] → O

The before-and-after design is very popular. But it gives no information on what may have caused any differences that result.

The input-process-output model

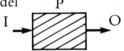

Now the progress (output less input) of pupils can be related to what went on in school.

The context-input-process-output model

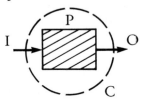

Now environmental factors can also be taken into account at input and output, and progress attributed to the school.

The most important feature of recent studies of school effectiveness (see for example Mortimore *et al*, 1988) is that effectiveness is detected when the progress of children is measured, not just their attainment. The distinction is crucial. Attainment refers to measures at output or input, aggregated to give a picture of attainment in a school. When this approach was used in large-scale studies the results usually showed few school effects. Attainment resulted mainly from factors in the social background of the children. But by assessing individual children at the start and finish of schooling, their progress can be measured. Then the effect of schooling in 'value-adding' can be detected. This is particularly important as the Education Reform Act of 1988 introduces published attainment scores for schools. A school in a poor area is liable to have low attainment, even though it may achieve considerable progress among its children. A school in a rich area may have high attainment, but have done little to progress its children.

We should always look for the model used in the research or inspection. For example, Gray and Hannon (1987) identify four very different approaches used by HMI to interpret the examination results of schools. Using HMI reports of full inspections, they show how school results were interpreted very differently because there was no agreed model in use. For example, the context of the school was only taken into account for schools facing pronounced advantages or disadvantages. Researchers are also prone to use very different models. Many early evaluations of traditional against progressive primary schools, or selective against comprehensive schools are unreliable because they used only output or input-output designs (see Shipman, 1988).

The limitations in the evidence

The evidence from school and teacher effectiveness studies does not enable a blueprint to be produced. The researchers examine those factors that are readily observable or measurable and those to which they can obtain access. For example, it is rare to find direct evidence on the quality of the teachers because few LEAs, teacher unions or school staff would agree to allow competence to be examined. Hence this factor does not appear directly in the list of factors found to be important. Surrogates such as the need for improved initial or in-service training do however appear as indirect ways of saying that teacher quality is not all it should be.

Even more important, each of the factors identified as contributing to school effectiveness may be very difficult to put into practice in a school. This difficulty can be seen in the collaborative exercise from 1982 to 1986, involving 14 countries in the International School Improvement Project (OECD, 1985). This project produced 6 books and 6 long technical reports. But it rarely seems to be concerned with learning and has had little impact on school organisation. It is difficult to see how many factors identified as important could be implemented.

The danger in the evidence

Evidence on attainments is related by researchers to factors in the social background of children as well as to the organisation of schools. There is a danger in this which is even greater when the relation examined is between attainment and intelligence. Across the first 60 years of this century it was assumed that children were born bright or dull and that achievement was determined by this largely inherited potential. We know now that the evidence on which this was based was inadequate and supported by fraud (see for example Hearnshaw, 1979). Yet there is still staffroom talk of children born thick. Even more prevalent is the use of sociological evidence to relate poor attainment to social or cultural background. These assumptions share a determinism, a fatalism that cannot be supported by evidence. An effective school has high expectations for all children and avoids building deterministic assumptions into its organisation.

The factors in school effectiveness

Not surprisingly there is consistency in the findings on the factors in schooling that are associated with high attainment whether measured as output only or as progress by relating input to output. There are reviews from Britain (see for example Reid, Hopkins and Holley, 1987) and from the USA (see for example Pukey and Smith, 1983) that list very similar factors. The most recent studies (see for example Mortimore *et al*, 1988) tend to confirm these lists for primary as well as secondary schools. The differences in these studies are largely in the emphasis given to structure and to culture. The former focuses on organisation, usually observable, measurable practices. The latter is concerned with less tangible features such as ethos, climate and spirit. That difference in emphasis recurs in most studies of management where structure and culture, tight/loose properties, structural plan and corporate spirit, scientific management and human relations are recommended.

1 *Decision-making*
Here the concern is with the way decisions are made throughout the school. This concerns not only headteacher, but the part played by staff and the involvement of pupils and parents. The effective schools were well led, and teachers knew what was going on. The individual factors identified are as follows.

a *Leadership by the headteacher*
This usually comes top of any list of factors. It is also given prominence by HMI. The successful style was to establish goals and inspire others. It involved active involvement in the school, establishing policies that enabled teachers to perform effectively without excessive interference, yet gave the headteacher sufficient knowledge about what was going on around the school and in the classrooms.
b *The involvement of teachers*
In effective schools teachers had high morale, were involved in planning curriculum, the allocation of resources and in

forward planning. They felt empowered to influence organisation and curriculum. This meant that staff were involved
directly in decision-making and felt responsible for policies.

c *The involvement of parents*
High levels of parent–teacher and parent–headteacher contacts
were found in effective schools. The evidence is particularly
strong for primary schools. This factor has little to do with
formal arrangements such as parent–teacher associations and
most to do with informing, welcoming and involving parents
in the school.

2 *The management of learning*

Here the concern is with the curriculum and teaching that
produces the attainment measured in the research. The factors lie
behind the progress made by children and the evidence suggests
that an effective school is effective for all children, able as well
as less able.

a *High expectations*
Effective schools tended to have high expectations of pupils.
The teaching was intellectually challenging. The teachers
encouraged children to use their imaginations, to be creative.
They were stretched regardless of ability.

b *Work-related classroom environment*
Learning was promoted by teachers who kept children
motivated through a classroom that was not just busy, but
concerned with attainment. Time-on-task was high.

c *Maximum feedback to pupils*
Attainment was high where pupils received rapid and regular
feedback on their work. Teachers and pupils were in continuous
communication about the work in hand. In particular, pupils
knew how they were doing and received praise for good work
rather than punishment for bad. This is in line with the
psychological evidence which I discuss in Chapter 7.

d *Work was carefully planned, delivered and recorded*
In effective schools the teachers planned the curriculum
together and were careful to record the performance of pupils.
There was a structured pattern to work in primary schools
and a limited range of activities at any one time. Classroom

time was efficiently used. Homework in secondary schools was set, marked and followed up in a systematic way.

e   *Learning was managed*
Research into teaching has confirmed that learning is increased where work is planned and delivered by teachers who keep up the momentum, interact with pupils and keep them alert by questioning. That classroom management was focused in particular on progression and matching, ensuring that children were working with a feeling of success on a curriculum that kept them stretched.

3 *A favourable school climate*
Most studies conclude that a school ethos, climate or feeling is important. This is derived from observation or from reviewing other factors rather than by direct evidence. It suggests that HMI and researchers feel that a school is more than the sum of the individual factors studied.

a   *A positive climate*
Effective schools were pleasant to work in for pupils and teachers. Everyone felt appreciated and rewarded. There was a sense of purpose and agreement over goals. Staff and pupils took pride in belonging to the school.
b   *An orderly, consistent environment*
Effective schools not only felt pleasant to be in, but had established self-control among pupils. The staff behaved consistently and shared common values. Discipline was internal not imposed.

School and home

The progress of children may be influenced by the way they are taught, but their attainment will nevertheless tend to be closely related to their social background. The evidence on the influence of social class has been collected regularly for over 60 years (Lindsay, 1926). It is based on three types of crude data. Some stays at the level of material factors such as father's occupation or income, or type of housing. Some goes beyond this to examine attitudes towards schooling. There is also evidence that generalises about the cultural background of children. All show that home factors have an important impact on attainment. Indeed, social background, however crudely measured is the best predictor of a child's performance on tests and examinations at any one time.

The difficulty in going beyond correlation towards explanation can be seen in the history of attempts to pinpoint causes. These attempts come and go. Material deprivation was seen as the problem. But sophisticated studies showed that parental attitudes outweighed material conditions (see for example Douglas, 1964). Subcultural theories assumed that school and home often have contrasting values and that this accounts for the lack of impact of schooling among identifiable groups. For others the differences are accounted for in the way language is used in different social class or ethnic groups. More recently the focus of research has been on the provision in schools rather than the circumstances of the children. However, if tests and examination results are accepted as important indicators, the importance of environment has to be accepted, despite the difficulty of moving from correlation to causation.

While there is a long history of research on the effect of social class differences on attainment, other bases for identifying groups who were losing out in education were overlooked for many years. However, the evidence on sex and race differences has accumulated recently and today class, sex and race form the three bases for identifying groups whom the schools seem to fail. With this view the limitations of much early evidence is apparent. Classifying children by race, class and sex shows a variety not found in most of the available studies (Tomlinson, 1984). As the evidence has been accumulated, so the view that the social background 'caused' the low attainment has been replaced by examining class, sex and race bias in schooling in all its complexity.

The implications of this evidence for management are very important. Identifiable groups of children are prone to lose out in school. The statistical evidence may be difficult to interpret but it is a warning that school management should not ignore the injustice that may be present. There should be monitoring to ensure that the position is known. In many schools and LEAs there are policies to eliminate racial or sexual bias in schools.

Ensuring that teachers are aware of the issues and motivated to help has become a priority for school management. Schools can be effective. But they need to be user-friendly to girls, to black children, to the poor, and to those with special needs.

There is another even more important factor in home-school relations when the focus switches to learning itself. It has been stressed repeatedly in this book that management is ultimately a means to secure entitlement for all children to high standards of learning. It takes management into the learning process itself. That is touchy ground. Not even the 1988 Education Reform Act says anything about pedagogy except to confirm that it is the task of the teachers. Yet teachers can only exercise their right to organise learning in their way, in their classrooms, for their children, if the conditions for learning are managed. Some schools receive children ready and keen to learn. Some have staff exhausted by the effort to keep children in some sort of order where learning may occasionally be possible. Most teachers work hard to establish the conditions where learning has priority. The management of learning cannot be assumed. It should be central to school management training. The management of learning should provide teachers with conditions under which they can concentrate on pedagogy. They should feel supported, should feel that they are working together. So should the children. So should the parents.

This view results partly from the finding that effective schools have obtained the support of parents. The most telling evidence comes from studies of young children (see for example, Tizard and Hughes, 1984). They list five factors that make the home an effective context for learning. These were

- the range of activities is extensive
- the parents and children share experiences over long periods of time
- the child, or children, usually have the attention of adults to themselves
- the home is full of real situations of great importance to children
- the relations in families are close and often intense.

These important educational experiences are found in poor as well as wealthy homes. The children can join in the adult world and engage in dialogue with one or two adults. None of these conditions are easy to arrange in schools. The effective schools manage to involve parents, use the experiences in the home, individualise teaching. But the experience and the communication remains restricted in classrooms with many children and one teacher. The advantage does not cease because the child is at school from 5 to 16. Nor do the disadvantages. The intensity of life at home can be powerfully negative as well as positive. Given the close links between school and home in determining learning and the success of schemes to involve parents in raising attainment it is difficult to understand the low priority given to home-school relations in management training, particularly in secondary schools. There are exceptions (see for example Bastiani, 1987). But the general neglect of learning has also led to a neglect of influences on learning outside as well as inside the school. The 1988 Education Reform Act, linking together curriculum, assessment and more information to parents of school and individual attainment, provides an opportunity to redress this balance.

There are however different levels of involvement. The 1988 Act will ensure that parents receive information on attainment in the school and on their own children. This could still be organised to avoid their close involvement with teachers. By then many schools will have thought about marketing to preserve their enrolment. But that would be to substitute a cosmetic for the chance to get parents behind learning in the school. Evidence and legislation have come together with teacher actions to give an opportunity to turn schooling into education.

The implications for school management

Teachers are right in viewing this evidence on school effectiveness with caution. First, the evidence that schools are effective in 'adding on' attainments, both in curriculum areas and in behaviour does not reduce the influence exerted by social background. Second, the factors selected for study exclude some that are possibly very important although difficult to research. The most obvious is the quality of teaching. There are no agreed criteria of good teaching. The evidence on the effectiveness of teaching styles is contradictory. We do not know how consistent teachers are in their teaching over time and with different groups of children. We know from intensive classroom studies that children often

at is going on in ways that differ from the intentions
er (see for example Woods, 1980). But we have only
to relate particular teaching styles to particular pupil
yles and are a long way from knowing how one
:o the other (see for example the ORACLE project
n Galton and Simon, 1980).

Third, there is difficulty in sorting out which of the factors
behind school effectiveness are means and which are ends. Strong
leadership, a good climate, high expectations and so on can be
taken to be ends as well as means. All the factors listed may
be individually worth aiming for. The difficulty is to establish
widespread involvement in decision-making or consistency among
teachers or full use of the time for work in the first place. Indeed
a school with these characteristics would hardly be bothered
about its effectiveness. Most of the factors are desirable ends in
themselves. This points to the danger in assuming that the factors
cause the effectiveness. The test would be to predict first, then
introduce the factors and then measure the gain in attainment.
That is rarely possible. Researchers therefore tend to rely on
assessing attainment first, then tracing differences back to the
organisation of schools. That *ex post facto* approach is unsatisfac-
tory. There is no way of knowing the combination of influential
factors around the school at the time when they were influential.
Schools can be effective this year but not next. We are a long way
from having the key to effectiveness through the application of
some combination of practices in school and classroom.

The most important contribution of school effectiveness studies
to school management is in the priority given to learning as the
end. They are an antidote to seeing schools as ends in themselves
and to evaluations that focus on processes without a look at
whether they are leading to improved attainment. They point to
the importance of leadership, but also to consistency among the
staff and of a feeling of being listened to and valued. That also
applies to parents and pupils. The effective school is not just a
tightly run organisation with a strong senior management. It is a
place where all those involved are actively pulling in the same
direction. It is a place where bottom-up initiatives are encouraged.
It is a place where external influences are welcomed and used for
internal advantage.

The evidence on school effectiveness also supports the use of the two contrasting models of decision-making outlined in Chapter 4. Effective schools have a clear sense of where they are going because there is leadership and involvement. They also have a clear idea of how they intend getting there. They are well organised and expectations are high. Decisions are made rationally by considering any available evidence, by considering the different views of staff and then moving to informed implementation. But effective schools also use the ideas that emerge from the day-to-day decision-making in the classroom, among the teachers. That is what involvement, empowerment, a good ethos, full communication across the school and from bottom to top means. That means a lot of wandering about by headteachers.

6 The evidence: curriculum development

School effectiveness studies yield evidence on factors that account for differences in attainment between schools. Studies of the curriculum yield evidence on factors in changing schools. Thus they complement one another. There is copious evidence available, largely from the 1960s and 1970s, when Schools Council and private sponsors such as the Nuffield Foundation resourced attempts to change the school curriculum. It was collected in a period when the curriculum was primarily the concern of teachers not politicians, and has to be interpreted in the light of that changed context. But it remains important. The National Curriculum has still to be implemented, in the complicated social organisations called schools.

The research reported here includes, not only studies of developments and the evaluation of their impacts, but descriptive surveys of the curriculum, studies of teaching and learning, and observations of schools as organisations. All these yield clues to why a National Curriculum is being introduced as well as how it can best be managed. Much of the research on the curriculum in the 1960s and 1970s painstakingly repeated work already completed in the study of organisational change by social scientists in earlier decades. Evidence from that older tradition is included to provide a firmer base for school managers faced with change.

Surveys of curricular provision

These surveys cover both primary and secondary schooling. The aim has been to plot the variety in provision across large samples of schools. In the primary school surveys the concern has been largely with timetable provision for the basic subjects of language and mathematics. In secondary schools the concern has been with option choices, usually to pick courses that will lead to different public examinations. The evidence exists at two levels. First, there are tabulations of the time allocated to subjects. Second, there is evidence on the way different children, or groups of children, receive very different allocation, even within the same classrooms.

In secondary schools, public examinations restrict the variety in curricular provision. The National Curriculum in the 1988 Education Reform Act merely confirmed a curriculum that had been remarkable for its consistency since the establishment of the Secondary Schools Examinations Council in 1920. There was however choice in the option system for the 14-year-olds. The evidence suggests that this served to confirm pupils' notions of their own abilities learned in the early years of secondary schooling (see for example Hurman, 1978). It also led to subjects being dropped, producing an unbalanced curriculum for many children in their last two years of statutory schooling and therefore problems when entering further education or work. HMI were also concerned about the balance of the curriculum, particularly for less able children aged 14 to 16 (DES, 1984). With falling rolls and free choice the results could be 'bizarre'. Breadth and balance in the curriculum were of increasing concern to HMI as they reviewed published reports on school inspections in the 1980s.

In primary schools, teachers had scope to establish their own priorities. It is easy to exaggerate the change that occurred. Innovation was emphasised in the Plowden Report (DES, 1967), but later surveys showed that in most schools very little change, except the movement to mixed ability grouping, had taken place across the 1970s (Boydell, 1981 and Barker Lunn, 1982). Nevertheless, teachers had organised very different learning experiences for children.

Three studies of the same primary age groups (Bassey, 1978; Bennett, 1980; Galton et al, 1980), give a timetabled range from under 10 per cent to over 40 per cent for mathematics, and from under 20 per cent to over 50 per cent for language. Similar variations have been found in other subject areas (see for example Shipman, 1985). Within these averages there were extreme individual cases. There are nursery schools where no writing is displayed for fear of children seeing it and being interested, while in others reading is taught formally. There are primary school classes where long division with remainders is still taught while in other classes of the same age, multiplication tables are not learned by heart (see for examples, Tizard, 1988). There is room for the individual in teaching, but it is not always to the benefit of children.

Studies of teaching and learning

Within classrooms, research has uncovered other variations Bennett et al (1980) and Galton et al (1980) have shown that some children are involved in work over 75 per cent of the time while others average below 30 per cent. While a topic may be on the timetable, some children never get around to it. Indeed, the evidence from the ORACLE project (Galton et al, 1980) suggests that one group of teachers, the 'habitual changers', gave little opportunity for children to get down to work before they were moved on to the next activity.

Research into junior school classrooms also shows that boys are liable to receive a different curriculum from girls, Blacks from Whites and working class from middle class children (see for example Mortimore, 1988). This difference does not show up on the timetable, but occurs through the grouping of children in the classroom. This also applies to very young children. Tizard et al (1988) have shown how infant school teachers have different expectations of boys and girls. In secondary schools the sex differences are stereotyped (see for example Stanworth, 1983).

This research into teaching and learning is focused on the gap between the intentions of teachers and the actual experiences of learners. In infant schools, Bennett et al (1984) have shown how the quality of pupil learning is affected by the way children assume that teachers want quantity not quality, so that efforts to promote high-order cognitive skills are reduced to copious writing and pages of sums. Galton et al (1980) have shown 'busyness' to be the most prominent feature of primary school classrooms, Southgate et al (1981) have shown the limited contacts between pupils and teacher despite the emphasis on individualisation in planning the teaching of reading. In secondary schools, HMI (DES, 1979) have shown that apparently simple regimes can be confusing from the pupils' point of view.

This evidence has a vital message for the management of schools. It cannot be taken on trust that even when there is a National

Curriculum, all children will share in it. Part of the problem arises from legitimate planning by the teacher to cater for individual differences. But part of it is unfortunate, unplanned and unnoticed. Management has to include the monitoring that can expose and hence lead to the correction of accidental inequalities, as well as review the curriculum that is on paper. At every age of schooling, the research has shown gaps between intention and reality. Of course that gap is expected and consequently probed by researchers. It may be exaggerated by neglecting evidence of aspects which are going well. But the gap remains an important focus for the management of schools.

This evidence was building up across the 1980s prior to the Education Reform Act in 1988. It was supplemented by the publication of HMI inspections of schools and by publications on the curriculum based on these. By the mid-1980s the pattern of HMI thinking, based on the evidence they had accumulated was clear (see for example DES, 1985a). There was to be a curriculum from 5 to 16 to which all children were entitled. It was to have breadth, balance, relevance, progression and continuity. It should also be differentiated, matched to the different capabilities of the children. These conclusions can be seen in the HMI surveys of the different age phases of schooling published earlier (see for example DES, 1978 for primary schools and DES, 1979 for secondary schools). Across the 1970s and into the 1980s, the academic evidence and the conclusions of HMI had established an agenda for school management that paved the way for the 1988 Education Reform Act.

School studies

Studies of schools as organisations have engaged sociologists for over twenty years. Ball (1987) lists 11 such studies written within ten years to 1987. Earlier books such as Hargreaves (1967) and Lacey (1970) became best-sellers. More recent studies have appeared as articles rather than books as their novelty decreased. They are mostly studies of secondary schools, focused on the rich social interaction resulting from pupil responses to school organisation. To Ball, these studies add up to a 'micro-politics' of the school. This view shows schools as places where headteachers,

teachers, pupils and parents manoeuvre to obtain power or protect their own position.

This evidence is important for school managers. It exposes the structure of the school within which decisions are made and implemented. It confirms the views of decision-making as a political process spelled out in Chapter 4. The intensive observation within schools shows up the conflicts, both hierarchically between headteacher and staff, teachers and pupils, and across departments, between teachers, among pupils. Those conflicts arise from very different views of what should happen in school. The evidence confirms that to speak of a school as having aims, policies and so on is not just to give it a group mind as if it was a person, but is to ignore the conflicts among those involved. The school is composed of different individuals and groups, each pressing their own case. This is of course the model of the education service as a whole presented in Chapter 4. Decisions come through conflict as well as consensus. So will curriculum change.

The conflict in schools is seen in these studies as having a distinctive, passionate, ideological nature. Apparently minor routine changes can be seen as a threat to equality or justice. Recommendations from town or county hall are often seen as violating the rights of teachers. The intervention of DES in the school curriculum is received as an attack on teacher autonomy. Many teachers, to their credit, are sensitive to anything that might make the position of chidren with special needs even worse. They suspect any innovations that might penalise those from minorities or increase sexual stereotyping. School management, particularly when it affects the curriculum has to work in an emotionally charged political atmosphere.

Finally, these school studies uncover the way the organisation of schools consolidates the conflict and the passion. One well-researched hypothesis is that streaming starts by separating the able from the less able and ends by polarising them (see for example, Lacey, 1970). That accounts for the way teachers have pressed for de-streaming, against advice from HMI and LEA advisors. Academic issues are mixed with social concerns. Schools and their curriculum are justifiably seen by teachers as important for the future life chances of their pupils.

Studies of curriculum development

The establishment of the Schools Council in 1964 marked the start of a remarkable period of attempts at planned curriculum change in England and Wales. Academia not only housed many of the 200+ projects, but established departments of curriculum studies and research. These flourished for about 20 years. They developed a number of models of curriculum change, and initiated many attempts to develop the curriculum and to evaluate the impact of these efforts. This was an international phenomenon and has resulted in a sizeable body of evidence on how schools change and how teachers respond to externally-devised moves to develop the curriculum. While this evidence is largely a tale of failures, it forms an important body of evidence for school managers, particularly as they struggle with changes imposed from outside schools by national or local government.

By the 1980s the evaluations of individual projects and programmes were available in the UK, in the USA, Australia and elsewhere. There were also authoritative reviews of these evaluations and of the experience of planned curriculum development. This section owes most to Fullan (1982) and Sarason (1982).

1 *The failure to conceptualise innovations*
The evidence on planned curriculum development suggests that very few developments had a lasting and intended impact. Indeed, many were never implemented in ways intended by those who designed them. This is a mystery until curriculum change is seen as one example of educational change in general, subject to political decision-making and taking place in schools which are rife with unintended consequences and with the passionate concern of teachers for justice. Very few plans achieve their promise. Very few panaceas achieve very much. Very many breakthroughs end as dim memories. Failure to implement is common. The obvious response to this waste of effort has been to look for the faults in the procedures for implementation. But there are prior explanations.

a *Many of the proposals were best left unimplemented*
Many curriculum projects either lacked desirable goals or failed to specify them. Innovations are means to ends, not ends in themselves. The curriculum development industry was

established to get changes into the schools. These developers often treated innovation as an end in itself. Teachers either rejected the package, let the effort lapse after a trial period, or merged the innovation into their ongoing work. This was reasonable behaviour. They were safeguarding the future of their pupils as well as getting back to routine.

b   *Most developments were marginal.*
Most projects left the main body of the curriculum untouched. They were especially concerned with humanities, integrated studies, social education and new ways of teaching old subjects. They were often seen as threatening to mainstream subject teachers. They were suspected by parents, particularly if they seemed to threaten examination results or time spent on basic subjects in the primary schools. It is significant that the most successful Schools Council project in terms of impact was Breakthrough to Literacy (Schools Council, 1979). The majority of projects were barely remembered when impact was investigated.

c   *Important curricular issues were ignored*
The list of Schools Council projects from 1964 is remarkable for its diversity. But it is also notable for what was left out. The Council came very late to the disadvantages of girls and Black children. It persisted in funding projects that had the effect of differentiating between the able and the less able and thus between the rich and the poor.

d   *The curriculum was seen as a collection of disconnected parts*
When the Schools Council did consider the total curriculum offered to children it produced excellent work (see for example Schools Council, 1981). But by the time it got to the centre of the curriculum, it was pre-empted by HMI and central government publications on the curriculum (see for example, DES 1977a). Curriculum evaluators in the 1980s, with the benefit of earlier evidence, came to focus on the relation of externally organised innovations to the whole school organisation. For example, two Education Support Grant funded projects into Lower Achieving Pupils (NFER, 1988) and Records of Achievement (DES, 1989) concluded by stressing that the new can not just be bolted on to the old. There has to be genuine adaptation to give the innovation a chance of working. School management cannot assume that

this will evolve. Getting the new integrated with the old takes time and effort. Curriculum developments have to be seen as new parts in a working whole. Integrating them means adjusting the mainstream. That is why internal developments often turn out to be the tortoises that win in the end.

2 *Problems in developing curriculum*

The educational problems in conceptualising innovations were behind many apparent failures to change schools. The 1960s and 1970s were the high point of teacher autonomy. It was difficult for curriculum developers to secure leverage because teachers often had their own conception of what education was about. But there was also a problem in implementing changes even when there was agreement. The change process itself was rarely considered, despite the copious evidence available on organisational change. It was very difficult to persuade curriculum developers in the 1960s and 1970s that social scientists had been there before in the management of change. This existing evidence pointed to the importance of appreciating both the meaning to the individual faced with change and of looking into the social complexity of the organisations in which it was to take place. The curriculum developers re-invented the wheel as they tried to change the curriculum. This also applied to curriculum theory and evaluation. Case study, illuminative evaluation, ethnography had been used in sociology for fifty years, but were ignored while curriculum theorists developed these methods without reference to past experience.

a   *Changes have different meanings for different people in different positions*
    Teachers see things from their classroom position. That means that they see a different change to that designed by a government working party, curriculum developer, inspector, advisor or committee, accepted by a headteacher, received by pupils and evaluated by parents. All will respond according to the meaning they give to events.
b   *Change is a long process, not a sudden event*
    Here we are back at the political model of decision-making discussed in Chapter 4. The decision to adopt an innovation is preceded by a long history of steady development and is

followed by a long period of implementation, if it survives. Thus the innovation has to fit into an existing curriculum in which teachers have a lot invested. Only the fittest developments will survive and even then are likely to be domesticated.

c   *Teaching is a private affair*
Curriculum change disturbs the privacy of teaching. It exposes teachers to new ideas and methods which can show up weaknesses concealed by following routine. Involvement in curriculum development often means visits by inquisitive outsiders. INSET only makes any weaknesses more public. This aspect is rarely discussed, but the problem may initially be the quality of teaching, not the curriculum. Changing the latter is going to do little good. Development has to take these sensitivities into account. The more enthusiastic and radical the innovator, the more threat to the teachers.

d   *Curriculum development needs support*
Change is eased if the rewards outweigh the punishments. Teachers in particular feel the lack of time to do their work. They shudder when the next innovation is foisted on them because it means yet another job to do. Yet there are rewards in being involved in change. The pioneers tend to make reputations and get promotion. Innovation brings rewards. But the punishment is not only felt in extra work, worry and exposure to outsiders pressing the change. It can come from colleagues who find that they too have to adjust, from pupils whose routine has been disturbed and parents who are worried about the effect on their child's prospects. Nor is this balance of influences on teachers easy to calculate for those wanting to promote change. The maintained system is in competition with the private sector. Parents and others are looking at the opportunity costs of innovation. If the school takes up this it gives up that. It may not be worth it.

e   *Small investments rarely yield big returns*
There is little evidence on this point because it has been neglected. Yet many innovations had big expectations and small budgets. Even at the end of the 1970s, with a decade of experience of under-funded projects there were proposals to improve education that were laughable in their ambition. I can remember £10,000 of Inner City Partnership money being proposed in Inner London for the improvement of the

teaching of Asian languages. This worked out at a few hundred for each language. This is not to claim that large investments necessarily pay off. Many large-scale American intervention programmes flopped. This was mainly because they were never properly implemented (see Berman and McLaughlin, 1978). But big money gives a chance of success. Most projects failed but they should not have been expected to succeed. Two examples of success following sufficient investment are described later in this Chapter.

f *Developments don't come one by one*
The stress caused by coping with simultaneous innovations has built up in the late 1980s. The 1988 Education Reform Act was exhausting because it contained the radical and related changes discussed in Chapter 2. But the Act was only another source of demands on teachers that had not only accumulated over the 1980s, but were being given little time for implementation. The period of consultation over proposed changes has been progressively reduced to about a month, often across a vacation period. Yet this isn't a new situation, even if the pressure has increased. Many Schools Council projects foundered in the 1970s because they coincided with raising the school leaving age and the reform of public examinations. The management of simultaneous innovations is a difficult if familiar phenomenon.

The 1960s and 1970s saw worldwide attempts to plan curriculum change. Church and state, priest and teacher have always tried to adapt the curriculum to new circumstances. In the 1960s and 1970s however, investment produced vested interests in planned change. Most apparent were the academics, working on curriculum projects and programmes, but also establishing departments of curriculum in higher education. There were also DES officials, HMI, local advisors, inspectors and advisory teachers, teacher centre wardens, consultants, publishers, researchers, research agencies such as the National Foundation for Educational Research (NFER) and individual teachers obtaining qualification through Masters and Diploma dissertations. The Schools Council (1964 to 1984) funded nearly two hundred projects. Curriculum evaluation became a major employment for educational researchers. It would be extraordinary if the evidence from that investment was of no significance for the management of schools, particularly the management of change.

In the 1980s the effort to change the curriculum has continued, but with a new style. The DES has used ESG money to set up pilot projects. Nearly £100 million was spent in this way in 1986–87 and 1987–88. The projects included some that continued the earlier interest in social responsibility, educational needs in a multi-ethnic society and developing oral skills. But the big money went on teaching science and mathematics, information technology and introducing GCSE. By the end of the 1980s the National Curriculum had been introduced. All these more recent developments have had evaluation built in as part of the contract for funding.

It is necessary to be cautious about drawing together this evidence to reflect on management, particularly of change, but it remains the most important we have. The first caution is that it contains a lot of contradiction. Secondly, reviews tend to use evidence from Britain, the USA and Australia as if the contexts for change were similar. Thirdly, and most important, they are summaries of 'planned' change. They assume that it can and should be managed. But it is possible to argue that this is to accept a mechanical, instrumental view of education (see for example, Holt, 1987). It is possible to argue that this is a technocratic approach while the real heart of education is humanistic. On this latter view the teachers should determine the curriculum. We should not be aiding governments to do the wrong job more effectively, but fight to stop the imposition of curriculum from above.

Has planned change been successful?

Most writers, including Fullan, Sarason and Holt, assume that planned curriculum change has been a failure. So do most in authority in education in Britain. Hence the move to a National Curriculum. But this is to take a narrow view. The Schools Council projects did have a small direct impact (Schools Council, 1979). The programmes set up by its successor, the Schools Curriculum Development Committee have received little publicity. Nuffield mathematics and science, initially hailed as major reforms, appear to have been absorbed and diluted. But the majority of projects were defined so broadly that success and failure are very difficult to distinguish. Curriculum outcomes are the heartland of unintended consequences. The impact of projects and programmes may have been considerable, but not as intended. The evidence of failure is mostly American (see for example, Berman and McLaughlin, 1978). Another way into the evidence to extract messages for management is to look closer at cases which did have an impact.

The Industrial Fund and science in the public schools

It was clear by 1960 that scientific and technical knowledge was going to be the key, not only to national economic and military strength, but to individual advancement in employment. The launch of Sputnik I by the Russians in 1957 is always given as the reason for the investment in planned curriculum in mathematics and science in the USA. In the UK, the Nuffield Foundation started funding development projects in Science in 1962. The Nuffield Science Teaching project provided a model for the Schools Council established in 1964. By this time it was clear that if schools that were competing for high-prestige employment were to hold their place, they could no longer rely on the traditional curriculum. Even the universities were dropping Classics as an entry requirement and were investing in science, mathematics and engineering departments.

The immediate response came from the public schools that depended on maintaining their relative advantage in obtaining university places. They received immediate and generous support from industry. The Industrial Fund for the Promotion of Scientific Education in Schools was established just as the Schools Council began its work (Glennerster and Wilson, 1970). ICI, Shell, ESSO, Vickers, and other large firms contributed about £3 million. This was used to launch appeals which raised about £16 million. Within a decade many boys' public schools had changed the balance of their curriculum and built new laboratories and workshops. In some schools Classics, once dominant, particularly at sixth-form level, shrank to a minor subject. Mathematics and science expanded to take its place. By 1970 the 104 boys' public schools that had received Industrial Fund money were producing 40 per cent of all science specialists entering universities. It is unfortunate, although understandable that this highly effective curriculum development has never been considered by those interested in innovation, because it illustrates what was wrong with the efforts at innovation in the maintained sector.

Five factors can be picked out for the success of the Industrial Fund. There was a lot of money. Allowing for inflation, the £20 million in the 1960s was far more than any innovation received in maintained schooling. Second, this money mainly came from fund-raising by the schools, with the external funding as a trigger. Third, the development was within the mainstream of the curriculum, geared to public examinations and becoming important in the job market. Fourth, it strengthened the position of the teachers affected by giving them extra resources without disturbing their teaching specialism. Lastly, the development had the support of parents, employers and admissions tutors in universities. These five factors are not found in the innovations established by the Schools Council. They are a combination of material support and enhancement of prestige that is unusual but significant for the management of change.

The Technical and Vocational Education Initiative

TVEI was announced in 1982. £10 million was allocated from the Manpower Services Commission to set up ten pilot programmes for 14+ year-olds in secondary schools. This announcement by the Prime Minister was received with loud complaints by the LEAs who had not been consulted over a major intervention into the secondary school curriculum by a Commission responsible to the Department of Employment, not Education, 'Fundamental constitutional questions' were at stake, according to the Association of County Councils (Times Educational Supplement, 19 November, 1982). Authorities such as the ILEA refused to bid for MSC money on grounds of principle. Yet by 1985 there were 74 projects and from 1987 all schools and LEAs could join.

The context of this spread is the appalling history of failure to provide a motivating curriculum for the 14+ group who would not take a full range of public examinations at 16. The school leaving age had been raised to 16 in 1972–73, but without any accompanying curriculum change. Producing an appropriate curriculum for the lower-attaining 40 per cent had been a priority for the Schools Council. Yet at the end of the 1980s there were still projects such as the Lower Achieving Pupils Project (LAPP) being funded direct by DES to produce models for reform. For ten years before TVEI was established the secondary school curriculum defied innovators, bored half the children and made life a misery for many teachers.

There was however a direct vocational objective behind TVEI. Since the end of the World War in 1945 there have been successive attempts to establish systematic industrial training in Britain. Everyone saw the need, given poor industrial performance, but the successive Acts had little effect. The Employment and Training Act of 1973 established the Manpower Services Commission with the funds and the clout to get some movement. By the end of the 1980s it had been a major force in curriculum development in schools as well as in the training of school leavers through the Youth Training Scheme. But it is wrong to see TVEI as restricted to vocational preparation only. Even though the extension of TVEI was funded at a less generous level than the first phase pilot studies, it was seen by many LEA as 'about whole-curriculum change for all students 14–19 in every secondary school and college within the LEA' (Cooper, 1988). After fifteen years of ineffectual curriculum development, TVEI was breaking the mould.

Evaluations of TVEI have generally been positive (see for example NFER, 1987). It brought resources into schools that had been economising hard for a decade. The 1987 extension was given £900 million over ten years. A look at the reasons for the success of the Industrial Fund shows how this largesse at a time of constraint reinforced other key factors. TVEI made the money allocated to previous ROSLA programmes look like peanuts. But it was also a chance for teachers to use these resources to build a new curriculum area, using modules out of other subjects, and relating this to employment. It had the support of partners and employers because it sounded and looked relevant to work at a time when unemployment was high. It provided a new set of career prospects for teachers at a time when promotion was difficult to obtain. However, it is also necessary to look at the organisation of TVEI to account for its success. Applications to join were made by proposals to MSC. These had to meet specified criteria. If successful, there was a contract issued that laid down procedures to be followed. The projects were evaluated both locally and nationally. There were TVEI advisors and units established to ensure that the schemes were well managed. This was a major investment of money and personnel. Furthermore, many schools were using it across the ability range. It has many critics who see it as an attack on a liberal education. But it had achieved a momentum beyond that of any other curriculum development aimed at the older secondary pupil.

The relevance of curriculum evidence for the management of schools

Many of the problems with developing the curriculum were managerial. Indeed, the factors listed above as important for determining the success of innovations are also those discussed in Chapter 1 as marking schools as organisations. Ends were confused with means, marginal was confused with mainstream, the limits on rationality due to lack of information and contrasting interpretations of that available were rarely appreciated by those pressing for change. Above all, many of the innovations threatened rather than promoted learning. Part of the management of schools has to be to secure sufficient stability to ensure that learning can take place. Too many changes coming too fast with insufficient resources can damage the organisation and expectations that ensures effective learning. In retrospect, objections to proposed changes in curriculum were usually seen by those promoting them as traditional defensiveness. For example, integrated studies ran into opposition from examination boards, subject teachers and parents. Opposition included complaints of excessive movement and noise (Shipman, 1974). Looking back these were usually dismissed as reactionary. They could have been legitimate.

The combination of material and social factors behind the successes of curriculum development also lies behind successful management. Rewarding a workforce for repetitive, mechanical grind had its limitations. Treating the workforce as valued humans while keeping wages low also worked for limited periods only. Management has to take both material and human rewards into account. The evidence from curriculum development is reinforcing an obvious but often neglected feature of management. If you want an effective organisation you have to provide the right tools for the job, sufficient rewards and get the support of those who can produce the goods.

This conclusion applies in particular to the management of change. In schools as elsewhere there are barriers to altering the way things are done. They arise from the way curriculum is locked into examinations, into professional training and development, into the way schools are organised, teachers paid and promoted, parents satisfied and targets achieved. Change is always risky. It can expose the teachers involved to outside scrutiny. It can give them extra work and worry. It can disturb the routine of the classroom. It can produce anxiety among parents. Headteachers and those outside the school can often miss these negative factors. Innovations look different when viewed from headteacher's study or town or county hall, or the DES. That is why Fullan's book is titled *The Meaning of Educational Change* (Fullan, 1982). The key to successful innovation is ensuring that the teachers feel that the rewards at least match the disadvantages, for the children as well as for themselves. But an optimistic conclusion can be drawn from this evidence. It shows that curriculum change can be managed. Combined with the evidence on school effectiveness it shows that learning can be promoted. Chapter 7 looks directly at this evidence on learning.

7 The evidence: learning

If school management should be concentrated on learning, then the evidence from educational psychology should be central. Unfortunately, the hopes of the pioneers of that subject at the end of the 19th century have not been fulfilled. The elaboration of the subject over this century has produced conflicting and not often applicable evidence.

Here, the following criteria have been used to select evidence for the management of learning. First, the evidence should not depend on any prior assumption about human nature. Second, the evidence selected needs to have stood up to repeated investigation. Third, the evidence needs to be consistent when collected by a variety of methods in a variety of contexts. That means that laboratory experimentation with rats is suspect. But if repeated practice helps rats to remember, while humans also remember more with reinforcement following initial learning, children in school benefit from revision, HMI observe its importance through homework and lesson planning and the 'practice makes perfect' adage seems to work, there can be more confidence. Finally, the evidence has to be treated as a supplement to, not a substitute for, teacher judgement. Teachers work in particular conditions, often on complicated, long-term tasks, with very different children. This practical experience cannot be dismissed. It is different, not inferior to evidence from research.

Using these four criteria, seven factors for which there is evidence can be isolated for guidance in organising learning in schools (Shipman, 1985).

1 Learning can be organised

Even where there are assumptions, such as children being seen as the agents of their own learning, or as full of energy to enquire and find out, effectiveness can be enhanced by organisation. If this were not the case, schooling would be a waste of money. Even the Plowden Report with its view that '. . . the curriculum is to be thought of in terms of activity and experience rather than knowledge to be acquired and facts to be stored' was full of evidence on how teachers could best promote this active learning (DES, 1967, para 529). Indeed, more organisation is probably needed for this approach than for the subject-based, knowledge-orientated National Curriculum twenty years later.

2 *Learning can be an incremental or a unified process*
Learning theories divide into: those where parts are built up from trial and error, stimulus-response methods until the whole is learned; and those emphasising the insightful jump to understanding that then puts the parts into place. There is evidence to support both theories. Indeed, the behaviourist and holistic schools of psychology have disputed for a hundred years. In practice, in schools, both are essential. There is a place for rote learning and for the experience that leads to insight. The skill of the teacher is to organise both into a learning sequence that will lead to mastery of the skills, knowledge or concepts involved. The nature of the task and the characteristics of the children determine whether the start is with the parts or the whole.

3 *Learners do best when they know what they are doing*
This points to motivation as important. Experiments with animals can depend on starving them and then presenting food. The motivation of humans is easier if they know what is happening, where they are supposed to be going. The tasks should be within their capacity and of interest to them. The more responsibility they take for their own learning, the more likely it is they will keep trying. Intrinsic motivation is more powerful than extrinsic.

4 *Learning is enhanced by reinforcement*
Rewarding success and correcting failure through organising feedback, is a key to keeping the learning going forward. The conditions are spelled out later. Here it is important to stress that this is a neglected aspect of the management of learning despite the weight of the evidence available. This cannot replace the intrinsic motivation discussed in (3) above, but it is an important feature of learning in school.

5 *Practice and application help the learning to last*
Facts and skills can soon be forgotten. Practising them helps.
Concepts and more complicated learning are more likely to be
mastered if they can be applied by the learners. Children need
help to look for patterns and relations, and practice in searching
for understanding by themselves.

6 *Learning is negotiation as well as transmission*
This is the equivalent of the caution that curriculum or any other
change in school is a social process rather than an event. Children
usually learn in groups. They interact with teachers. They bring
their own histories with them and the learning process becomes
social as well as intellectual. That is why it is sensible to talk of
user-friendly education or relevance in the curriculum.

These six factors can be arranged into the simple, three-stage
model suggested by Bloom (1976). This model makes no overt
assumptions about human nature and few about the process of
learning itself. It is summarised in this diagram.

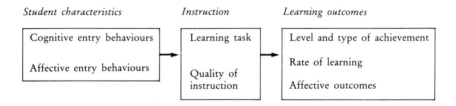

Bloom is primarily interested in the history of the learners and
the knowledge and the attitudes that they bring into the learning
situation. Thus the key to successful learning is knowledge among
teachers of that prior history. Secondly, Bloom is concerned with
the match between the tasks organised and the entry characteristics
of the learners. Here there is an assumption, indicated in the
outcomes. All children are assumed to be capable of learning,
although their mastery will vary in the level they can achieve and
the time they will take. Thus this is an optimistic and radical
model. It places responsibility for learning firmly with the teachers. But it is practical. It contains, for example, most of the
principles behind GCSE, the assessment of National Curriculum

and of much mixed-ability group teaching in the primary school. Above all, it focuses attention on factors that can be managed.

There is another important characteristic of Bloom's model. No assumptions are made about human nature. Nor are they about the relative contribution of nature and nurture. It is the entry characteristics of learners that matter. Obviously race, class and sex will affect these, but Bloom is saying that learning should be organised to take children as they are when it is about to take place. He is not ignoring the importance of social factors. Entry characteristics will include their influence. But he is saying that teaching should concentrate on effectiveness given the position reached by the children concerned and not give priority to social issues such as equality or psychological issues such as motivation. This is suited to a managerial approach. It is optimistic, because it assumes that all children can learn provided this is efficiently organised. It places responsibility firmly with teachers.

Evidence on the stages in learning

Psychology and common sense come together in seeing three stages in learning. First there must be a basis for further learning. Second, the learning needs to be organised to give learners the maximum chance. That means that there will be different rates of learning and differentiation in the tasks organised. Third, there needs to be some consolidation of what has been learnt. Preparation, carefully organised learning and reinforcement are the key parts of the process. Of course life is not that simple. A lot of learning is spontaneous. Learning doesn't occur in separate packages. Teachers may plan work in distinct parts, but children are learning all sorts of things at any one time, some supportive, some distractive. They are all bringing often very different experiences to bear. Much of the psychological evidence turns out to be unusable in schools because of this complexity in practice. It is difficult to follow psychological recommendations when thirty children are getting agitated. However, the Bloom approach does identify the key evidence for the management of learning and is free of romantic or reactionary views of children.

The conditions for learning

The evidence from school effectiveness studies for the importance of high expectations and a climate that emphasises learning is really pointing to the importance of teachers and learners feeling that something worthwhile is going on. Much of the information circulating within schools, between central and local government and schools, between schools and parents, employers and others in the community is about the importance of learning. From Secretary of State to classroom teacher, the rhetoric is designed to be motivating. The evidence supports the importance of this effort even if the gap between rhetoric and reality is wide. It is very difficult to explain the very high educational attainment of some national and religious groups without reference to different cultures of learning. Some attention has to be paid to the culture for learning in and around schools.

Attitudes are learned inside the school and outside. Frequently these are in conflict. The task of the teacher is to ensure that the positive outweighs the negative. That means that children can not be assumed to want to learn. That knowledge of affective entry characteristics is a basis for teaching. The incentives must be provided. Most of these tend to be long term. The prospect of good public examination results and hence a good job is unlikely to motivate a young child or one who is not good at academic work. Indeed, such a stress might put many children off working. Hence, incentives have to be realistic and tailored to individuals or groups of children. That of course is the reason for introducing Technical and Vocational Education into secondary schools, for differentiating the curriculum, for making it relevant. It also accounts for the efforts to involve parents.

This priority for attitudes, for motivation, is shared by teachers and psychologists. An example is the use of advanced organisers (Ausubel, 1963). Here the evidence is that the quality of work is improved if it is made meaningful by identifying and exploring key ideas in advance. At its most technical this involves identifying the main concepts in the work to be covered and introducing these to children as a preview. At the practical level it can be seen in the way teachers discuss what is to be done before they do it. The psychology of motivation and the activities of teachers share the same concern with getting learners ready to learn, hopefully enthusiastically.

The importance of motivation in learning accounts for attempts to make children more responsible for their own learning. Bloom makes no assumptions about motivation being natural. There is sufficient evidence to see it as open to organisation. Learning is improved if realistic targets can be set and responsibility accepted for reaching them. That lies behind much of the current stress on negotiation, on contracts, on formative assessment. If tasks are meaningless they will not be tackled with any enthusiasm. If learners know where they are supposed to be going they are more likely to try to get there. Better still, if they have some say in setting their own targets, agreeing to others and contracting to achieve a few the results are likely to come.

The investment in establishing positive attitudes towards learning can be justified by reference to psychological evidence as it can to the payoff in practice. The management problem is to find motivators for all children, particularly the less able, when most of the prizes go to the more fortunate. Differentiation in the curriculum and in assessment is however built into GCSE and into the assessment of the national curriculum. So is the realisation that some children will take far longer than others to reach specified levels of attainment. Further, the price of not investing in this effort to motivate is high. That is why the school effectiveness evidence includes emphasis on expectations. It also accounts for the current stress on the need to ensure that all children experience success. Teachers by themselves have limited scope to inspire. They need the support of other staff, of headteacher, of governors, of parents and others outside the school. Children will not work well if they, their parents and employers see work as a useless imposition.

Pupil, teacher and task

Most of the evidence on the organisation of teaching in the classroom is concentrated on the relation between the task in hand and the characteristics of the children. The psychological evidence suggests that teachers are right in aiming for a level of work that stretches children but is not too difficult. If it is too easy there is no point in it, if it is too difficult they will soon give up. HMI reach similar conclusions through their attention to the matching between tasks and children's abilities. Their concern that neither the more nor the less able were receiving an education that matched their abilities is a practical illustration of the same point (see for example DES, 1979). The task has to suit the capacity of children to master it, to match their cognitive entry characteristics.

The organisational problems raised by this need to match task and capacity arrive when the variety among children and the complexity of tasks are considered. In Bloom's model the learners are assumed to have histories resulting in them entering learning with distinctive knowledge, skills and attitudes. There is no reference here to ability. These cognitive entry characteristics can be assessed and are open to teaching. Affective entry characteristics include such personal attributes as self-concept, but also attitudes towards school and the task. The latter are once again open to influence by teachers. Similarly the teachers will consider the task and organise it so that children will have most opportunity to understand and the interest to keep working.

The psychological evidence on learning contains one feature that recurs, whether the models are incremental or holistic and the emphasis on rote or on understanding. The learning needs to be reinforced. Practice makes perfect. It is partly a matter of regular revision to aid memory. But it is also the result of children responding to success and benefitting from knowing when and how they have failed. Once again, no assumptions about needs or motives or drives are necessary. The evidence shows that if success in learning is rewarded quickly it tends to stick and promote further learning. Similarly failure can be inhibited by punishment, although here there are serious limits on this negative incentive. That simple view has of course been elaborated over a hundred years of experimentation in psychology, but it remains a guide to the management of learning. Schooling should offer every child success. That isn't easy, but without it schooling is a dismal prospect for many and in consequence the context for learning for all is disturbed.

There is a limit on the effectiveness of rewards to produce extrinsic motivation. They can undermine interest in learning in its own right, substituting the rewards for any interest in the subject itself. It is the building of intrinsic interest among pupils that is the real task of teachers. For that, pupils require information on what they are doing and why they are doing it. Building of interest points towards making pupils more responsible for their own learning.

The importance of reinforcement is curiously neglected in schools. Most assessment, by comparing one child's performance against that of others tends to be unrewarding to just those who need a boost. This norm-referenced information also gives little information that can be used to plan further work. It does not give data on the learning so far achieved. That accounts for the move towards criterion-refernced assessment. But conventional school assessments have also tended to be summative, coming at the end of a course, a term or a school career, with no time for reinforcement. Once again this accounts for the move towards formative assessment. Criterion-referencing and the use of formative assessment are principles accepted for assessing the National Curriculum. So is progression, the principle that the learning should be matched to the child's ability to learn, thus avoiding continual failure.

This sounds of course too good to be true. It is asking teachers to know the characteristics of their pupils as they progress through the curriculum. It is asking them to organise teaching so that these individual children can master the work through different tasks tackled at different rates. It assumes thorough assessment, recording and planning. The tracking of children from 5 to 16 up ten levels of about 50 Attainment Targets in the National Curriculum is going to lead to some unreliable assessment. But it will yield more information than has been available to teachers, pupils and parents to date. That assessment is justified in the 1988 Act by reference to raising attainment. That is also the concern of teachers as well as HMI. By reducing the model to the manageable, Bloom has provided an *aide-memoire* for reviewing the management of learning in schools that is in line with current thinking.

The outcomes from learning

To Bloom there are three dimensions of learning outcomes. One is the level and type of achievement. The second is the rate at which this learning is mastered. Both are open to management by teachers. The third is change in attitudes. Each of these forms the entry characteristics for the next phase of learning. There is nothing new in this. HMI stress differentation and relevance as two key characteristics of the curriculum (DES, 1985a). Differentiation requires knowledge of the entry characteristics of pupils and organisation of learning that allows for the different interests and work rates. Relevance is necessary because it has reinforcement built in. The National Curriculum is premised on the hope that children can progress up ten prescribed levels within Attainment Targets that define each subject of the curriculum. Different levels of attainment and different rates of learning are assumed. Secondary school teachers have learned to differentiate even among older children taking GCSE. Primary school teachers have grouped and arranged the curriculum to vary the expected outcomes according to the level of work at which children can cope and the speed at which they can do it.

Behind these prescriptions for varying the level, type and speed at which children will get through work are assumptions about the information that is available for the necessary planning. This was seen in Chapter 1 as a curious feature of schools. Management information going down was not necessarily influenced by information on learning coming up. Nor was the information from teachers on learning among children necessarily informed by management decisions. Indeed, the isolation of classrooms and, in secondary schools, departments, often produces teachers who pursue their own rather than any agreed curriculum and teaching style. The consensus that recurs in the evidence on school effectiveness is often missing. The management of learning has bounded rationality. Governors, senior staff and teachers act on limited information. This situation is intended to change with the 1988 Education Reform Act. The point is taken up again in Chapter 8 where the implications for the management of schools is related to the need for adequate information.

The amount of information demanded has been dramatically increased by the 1988 Education Reform Act. If teachers are to base their work on a thorough knowledge of the cognitive and affective entry characteristics of children from 5 to 16 it will require full recording, storage and retrieval arrangements. The steps expected are spelled out in the regulations for the National Curriculum. They include Standard Assessment Tasks, teacher assessment, Attainment Targets and records of achievement. Teachers will continue to keep their own records and will have to meet LEA requirements and report to parents and governors.

But the limited time and energy of teachers will have to be used effectively. The rationalisation of assessment procedures has to be a priority because assessment is the link between the learner and the curriculum, and the source of most of the information required at all levels, inside and outside the school.

The external influences on learning

So far learning has been considered within the school. But two sets of evidence widen the perspective. First, not only does a lot of learning take place in home and community, but these external factors affect what is learned in school. Second, much of this influence from outside the school is exerted through the social processes in learning. The evidence itself has been described in Chapters 5 and 6. Here it is only necessary to relate this evidence to that coming from psychology. The clue to understanding this relation has already been described in the distinction between attainment and progress. Schools have little control over the former but have responsibility for the latter. Home factors in particular account for levels of attainment achieved. But schools still receive pupils with particular entry characteristics and then add on learning. That definition of progress takes account of environmental influences.

The relation of this view of schools being responsible for progress is closely related to Bloom's model of learning. The emphasis on entry characteristics means that he could omit the different environments from which children came because they have already had their impact as they enter the classroom. That does not mean giving up the struggle to give all children a fair chance in life. It does mean that responsibility is firmly in the hands of teachers to ensure that children progress. We are back with determinism. That danger has been in the sociological evidence on the relation of attainment to social background as well as in the psychological evidence on the influence of heredity. The language of schooling and texts is full of 'poor backgrounds', 'inadequate parents', 'cultural deprivation' and 'poor self-concepts'. There is evidence that such interpretations are reciprocated by pupils seeing schooling as meaningless or demeaning (see for example Woods, 1976). The parties in the learning situation interpret events in very different ways, thus inhibiting learning.

The implications for management

The task for management in schools is to organise a context in which learning is encouraged. First, schooling should be 'user-friendly'. Race, class, sex and special need should not be the bases for children feeling under-valued or insulted. The relation to the influence of home, school and community on learning is close. It is not just the material conditions that influence learning. Indeed, the evidence suggest that these are less important than cultural factors. It is the latter that lead to conflicting definitions of the learning situation. Managing learning means looking across the boundaries of the school. The 1988 Education Reform Act, with the introduction of open enrolment, more powers to governors and parents, and more information for all parties places this firmly on the management agenda. But it is more than a matter of attracting customers. School management should always look first at the conditions for learning.

The second task of management is to ensure that learning is managed effectively throughout the school. That means putting the factors discussed above on the agenda for review. That is not an easy task given the claim to professional autonomy. It means allocating resources and hence establishing the priority for learning in the budget allocations. It means involving teachers in discussion of the progress of children and the relation between this, the curriculum and the reinforcement from organised feedback. A National Curriculum defined by Attainment Targets provides an opportunity for such a systematic approach. The assessment is mandatory and should not be wasted. It could provide pupils, parents as well as teachers with the information that will guide and encourage learning. The evidence in Chapters 5, 6, 7 confirms that learning can be managed. That is why schools can be effective.

8 The management of learning: getting the information

The distribution of information in education is often casual. As the flow of documents on the 1988 Education Reform Act turned into a flood, the fractures in the lines of communication were exposed. The DES to LEA, LEA to schools, headteachers to staff path for circulation was leaving many teachers uninformed about the curriculum they were supposed to be using after the start of the school year in 1989. A few teachers, many parents and most pupils have little idea of what and why things are happening around them. Some prefer not to know, but many teachers fret that they have not received publications essential for them to plan their work. At the same time, those who produced the documents in DES, NCC SEAC and so on, worry over the best ways of getting their reports to those who need to read them.

It is difficult to remedy this situation. The publications are expensive to produce, to copy and to circulate. It is often difficult to predict the demand. It is necessary to rely on busy people in LEAs and in schools to act as efficient post offices. Further, at each stage decisions have to be made about who should get the copies. Sometimes this means guesswork. Sometimes it means breaking publications into small samples for widespread distribution in the hope that the right people will get their copy. It can sometimes involve selection in order not to worry some people, inform others and keep others in the dark. Information can reinforce authority, ease management and provide the basis for initiative at all levels. Even holding back information for a few days gives those in the know an advantage. The use of information is central to the management of schools, as it is to all organisations.

This is not a new situation. Schools are the black holes for a lot of information. Every minister, chief education officer, inspector and advisor lives with the surprise that their treasured report has not been seen by those whose futures depend on it. Information rarely seems to reach the right people. Its collection and distribution are casually organised. Headteachers rarely share the task. There are personal advantages in that, but post-1988, it is an obvious candidate for delegation. Someone on the staff should be making sure that all important documents are available and that their location is known to colleagues.

This chapter collects together the current demands for information in schools and shows how these can be met. The use of this information is the subject of Chapter 9. The demands arise from the 1988 Education Reform Act and from ongoing teacher-led developments. In both cases information is required as a means to improve learning. An information system should never be an end in itself, however. It too is a means to learning. It needs to be reviewed and pruned as curriculum and teaching method are changed. The intention here is to lay out the mandatory demands for information and show how these can be met while providing a basis from which learning can be managed.

The importance of radical changes in the provision of information lies in the idea of knowledge as power. Authority, in schools as elsewhere, is largely determined by access to information not available to others. That was spelled out in the discussion on bounded rationality in Chapter 1. Information is distributed selectively to maintain control as well as to avoid overloading individuals. That role of information in the authority structure of organisations means that as the quantity and flow of information changes, so organisations change. The 1988 Education Reform Act lays great stress on making information on achievement widely available. It will alter the relationship between headteacher, governors, teachers, parents and pupils. That is really what the term 'information revolution' means. It is not the technology but the impact on organisation that is crucial. That theme is taken up in Chapter 9.

We are now at the heart of school management, asking the question: 'Is it possible to manage a school to maximise learning, even when the weight of externally imposed change is heavy?'. Information is seen as the key to an answer, as it is to the management of learning in general. Three steps are recommended for organising the information requirements in schools. First, the evidence that is required by pupils, parents, governors as well as teachers and the LEA must be identified. Who needs what, when and where has to be considered. Second, the demands for information must be laid out so that all teachers are aware of what is expected of them. Third, there must be a systematic circulation of information to ensure that inside and around the school, the key personnel can pay their part in the promotion of learning. The assessment of pupils will be the main concern, but as part of the total organisation of information that includes the evaluation of the school, the internal and external distribution of information, and its regular housekeeping and if necessary, pruning.

What has to be done?

The 1988 Education Reform Act demands information at three levels: on pupils, on school classes or year groups and on the school as a whole. The information on pupil attainment is to be provided for parents at four reporting ages and records of achievement will extend the scope 'across and beyond' the national curriculum. In practice, information at these three levels is required by pupils, parents and teachers as the responsibility for learning is extended to all three. Children learn best when they know what they are supposed to be learning, know how they are doing and have information on how to improve. That information is also required by parents. Further, it is required by teachers, who often do not know what other teachers are doing and consequently have only limited information on how to help children. That problem is not confined to secondary schools. It is the explanation of the extraordinary variety experienced by children in the same primary schools (see, for example Bennett, 1980).

The mandatory task of school management in the last decade of the 20th century is to get the National Curriculum into place, resource it efficiently and present it so that it is appreciated inside and outside the school. This reorganisation takes place in schools that already have procedures for coping internally and with demands for information from LEAs and examination boards as well as central government. Behind these organisational concerns is the obligation to give each child a broad and balanced curriculum. Yet even that could be a cosmetic exercise. To translate the national curriculum into effective and beneficial learning for all children means building on experience of the circumstances and style of a particular school in a particular area. It means building on the developments which teachers have already found to be most effective. It means using the evidence on effective schooling, on the management of curriculum change, on the optimum conditions for learning. It means the promotion, not the abandonment, of the school as having a distinctive reputation. Above all it means maintaining a focus on the priority to learning for all children. As the information required by the National Curriculum is put into place, it must also serve the management of learning.

Getting the national curriculum into place

The National Curriculum is spelled out in regulations that are legally binding on teachers in maintained schools. The core subjects and foundation subjects must be included as they are the entitlement of all children, unless they are specifically disapplied. The statutory regulations for these subjects cover three sets of information, as follows.

> 1 *Attainment targets* that set objectives for learning, specified in up to 10 levels covering the ages 5 to 16. These often contain multiple statements of expected achievements.

> 2 *Assessment arrangements* related to the 10 levels of attainments and the reporting ages of 7, 11, 14 and 16.

> 3 *Programmes of study* spelling out the essential teaching within each subject.

The specifications in the regulations are not intended to be detailed or to define the scope of each subject. Orders will be used to further specify, amend and update as necessary. The National Curriculum Council (NCC) and the Schools Examination and Assessment Council (SEAC) will give further guidance. Schools are expected to produce and update their plans for the implementation of the national curriculum, and to ensure that breadth and balance are not disturbed. Teachers remain responsible for work in their classrooms. How they organise their work is their business, but the National Curriculum is legally binding.

Working with statutory requirements in the curriculum is a new experience for teachers. Further, the regulations spell out monitoring arrangements to ensure implementation. These consist of three aspects, as follows.

1 *Information requirements* to ensure that parents and others know how the school is implementing the national curriculum.

2 *Complaints procedures* established by LEAs and approved by the Secretary of State to enable parents and others to pursue their concerns about the way schools have implemented the curriculum. In addition, the Education Act of 1944 also allows for complaints direct to the Secretary of State.

3 *Monitoring* is the responsibility of LEAs through their inspectors. That has always been their statutory responsibility.

The orders introducing the National Curriculum, its assessment and the information to be made available to the public are being introduced as working parties and research teams complete their work, as the NCC completes consultations and as the Secretary of State places the Orders before Parliament. It will be a long and continuous process. It will not stop when the last Order is made to complete the National Curriculum. The Act allows for Orders to be used to develop the curriculum further. The National Curriculum is specified as a necessary basis for a complete curriculum, but other areas, such as careers, health and personal and social education have been identified as necessary additions for all pupils, and the subjects specified as foundation subjects are not seen as exhaustive. Religious education is still compulsory. Above all, each school is supposed to offer a distinctive curriculum. Indeed, the Act was criticised by those who support moves to take schools into a competitive, market situation for seeming to impose a standard curriculum that restricted their capacity to offer consumers, parents, a really differentiated product.

The provision of performance indicators

Management consultants looking at school in the light of provisions for local management of schools (LMS), emphasise the need for '. . . information provision to lie at the heart of a successful LMS scheme.' (Coopers and Lybrand, 1987). It is needed for

strategic, budget and timetable planning, for control and administration, for monitoring and feedback and for reporting on performance. This will require information from LEA to schools and
from schools to LEA, as well as information for management.
This will consist of financial, resource and output information.

There is a problem with performance data, particularly when it
is related to that on the running of the school. For example, staff
demeanour is recommended as a process variable with pupils'
demeanour, behaviour and attainment as outputs (Coopers and
Lybrand, 1987). The world of performance indicators includes
odd assumptions. Yet much of the information recommended for
collection will be of use to teachers as they put the published
assessments for the school into context and as they justify expenditure. Anything that is collected will need to be scrutinised to see
if it can be used to make data on learning more meaningful.

Continuing to meet externally derived demands
Schools have to cope with simultaneous innovations. Typical
was the introduction of a national curriculum and local financial
management just as the first year of the GCSE was completed.
Many secondary schools were also engaged in developing the
Technical and Vocational Education Initiative into an institutionalised part of schooling. Primary schools were busy implementing
LEA-produced curriculum guidelines, while worrying about
working party reports on the foundation sujects of the national
curriculum. Most schools were also involved in innovations, many
financed by Education Support Grants, such as teacher appraisal,
records of achievement, teaching science in the primary school or
improving the quality of education for primary children in both
urban and rural areas. All of these demanded the collection of
more information.

The need to cope with overlapping changes of the accompanying
demands for information was particularly difficult in primary
schools. Here the impact of the National Curriculum, with its
emphasis on assessment, was heavy, particularly as teachers in
Key Stage 1 were not only unused to a formal curriculum and
assessment but were the first to pilot standard assessment tasks.
There was no experience of external moderation of assessments
and the traditional view was that early formal assessment was
likely to be damaging to young children. These developments

came on top of LEA activity to increase the amount of testing for screening and monitoring (Gipps and Goldstein, 1983).

The organisation of information

The collection, storage, retrieval, organisation and circulation of information is already a major task in schools. New developments are adding to the strain. The production of records of achievement from 14 to 16 turned out to require often unavailable teacher time, storage space and secretarial support. So did the organisation of GCSE with its coursework components and complex assessment arrangements. Yet much of the information required for one was required for the other. Similarly the teacher assessments that will play the major part in allocating pupils to the ten levels of attainment on Attainment Targets in foundation subjects of the National Curriculum are not new. As they are put in place they will overlap with existing continuous assessments. LEAs are already working with schools to ensure that there is no clash or excessive waste of effort.

Two developments point to a way forward. First, the National Curriculum is defined by attainment targets and assessment is along ten levels for each. As a child moves through the Attainment Targets from five to 16 the progress will be assessed and recorded by teachers. At the four reporting ages, some combination of Standard Assessment Task and teacher assessment will be used. Thus for each pupil there will be a progressive record of levels achieved on the attainment targets for each subject area. Teachers will record when pupils reach a particular level. This will be a substantial task. Science and mathematics have some 30 Attainment Targets between them. At any one time there will be a full record of where a child has reached on these targets in all subjects, across the National Curriculum. This mandatory development may be unwelcome and it may lack validity, but it does provide a ready-made and nationally-backed assessment and recording system.

Second, it is intended that records of achievement shall be produced across the school career of all pupils from five to 16. Hence the formative assessments accumulated can form the basis of a running record for pupils that will follow them through their school career. The national guidelines for records of achievement among the 14 to 16 age group described them as giving coherence to schools' assessment practices (DES, 1989). Clearly if the progress of each child is to be recorded from five to 16, there will be no point in having more than one recording system. Reports to parents will be made at least once a year.

Thus the key issue is the relationship between assessment of the National Curriculum and the organisation of records of achievement. Each is intended to cover the statutory schooling of all children. Each is intended to be mandatory. Each will involve reporting to parents. The National Curriculum reporting ages of 7, 11, 14 and 16 are fixed. The summative record will become the property of the school leaver on leaving at 16. Interim summative documents will be issued if a pupil moves to another school, when requested by careers officers or employers. Bringing these two systems together will be crucial. Significantly this was the major point of the consultations undertaken by SEAC at the request of the Secretary of State, after receiving the national guidelines for records of achievement in 1989. It is possible that in time much of the information required for recording and assessment will be computerised, but a lot will have to be filed manually. To date the scope for using computers has been limited. In recording achievement they tend to narrow the information down to grades, or comment banks. The National Steering Committee for Records of Achievement came down against this restriction and employers supported them (National Foundation for Educational Research, 1989).

Who organises the information?
The recommendation of the Records of Achievement National Steering Committee was that a senior member of staff would be needed as coordinator for this initiative in schools. That is a common recommendation. Given the number of initiatives, there are unlikely to be enough senior staff to go round. Thus part of the review of information needs to address the question 'Who does it?'. At present only a minority of secondary and middle schools seem to have a coordinator of assessment (Clough, 1984). There are likely to be coordinators for records of achievement, for collecting data for reporting on achievement in the National Curriculum, examination officers, as well as form teachers, pastoral

staff and careers staff collecting their own information. Someone has to pull all this together and ensure that the maximum of information is available at the minimum cost of teacher time and effort. Whoever gets the job must have the authority to collect the information and the resources for filing, secretarial support, analysis and publication. It will be a major but essential task.

The management of information will bring the teacher or teachers responsible into close contact with governors. They have legal responsibility for the aims of the school and its curriculum. They need a flow of information. There will also have to be close contacts with LEA inspectors as they monitor the implementation of the National Curriculum, and with whoever has responsibility for accounting under Local Financial Management. Nor is this just an administrative task. The management of information has to be involved with the way learning is organised. The introduction of systematic recording and National Curriculum assessments starts with the reorganisation of the curriculum and the way teachers go about their work. It has to reflect the values built into teaching in the school. The information will have to be analysed and used to advise school management on strengths and weaknesses. It will be a sensitive as well as crucial task. That is why a review is the first step. Staff will have to have confidence in the person as well as the system.

How is it to be kept up to date?

The perils of storing data lie in the cobwebs accumulated. Too much of it is collected and not used in schools. In many cases a regular review of each child's progress would have better results than the storage of unused data. Even LEAs collect test results and then never use the information (Gipps and Goldstein, 1983). The reason is often that the real reason for getting teachers to test or report is to ensure that they are doing their job of reviewing pupil progress, rather than any real interest in the data itself. A regular review of information can at least bring this issue into the open. But it is also necessary to organise regular housekeeping to prune out the superfluous data and cease collecting it. That is especially important as new demands for information are met. Hopefully LEAs will limit their demands on schools as National Curriculum assessment increases. But headteachers also need to encourage spring cleaning.

How is it to be related to the development of the school?

Information is central to decision-making in schools as elsewhere. As the school develops, the demands for information will change. Thus the review of information should not be separate from school review as a whole. If a school has institutionalised self-evaluation, that is the place for such an information review. That will lessen the chance of it being seen as an isolated aspect. This point has been reiterated throughout this chapter as elsewhere. Putting learning at the centre means relating management to areas which are often protected as the concern of teachers alone. It means treating the school as a whole. That is the message of school effectiveness studies and the reference to school climate, to consensus, to shared expectations. It is the consequence of the post-1988 market position of schools. It is the rationale behind local financial mangement. The school is to be judged as an organisation. It will have to be managed as one. That makes it very difficult to assert the independence of teachers in the organisation of learning once it becomes the focus of management.

9 The management of learning: using the information

The theme of this book is that training for school management has strayed from giving priority to learning by concentrating on administration rather than the encouragement of initiatives to raise attainment. The focus on information arises from that concern. Teachers are most active around the learning they organise. That is where they can change, and have changed, the education system. But the opportunities to exert influence depend on being informed and having the motivation to take initiatives. An accelerated programme of reform imposed by central government has exhausted many teachers. Yet the Education Act of 1988 is premised on the assumption that teachers will not only implement a National Curriculum but continue to develop it.

This assumption of continuing enterprise seems macabre in many schools wrestling with the complexity of the imposed changes at the start of the 1990s. Yet development will continue and the teachers will still influence it where it matters: where children learn. Here the demands of the Act meet the interests of teachers. Schools are being reorganised, not just to produce a national curriculum, locally managed, but to prepare and release information previously protected as confidential in the classroom. The 1988 Education Reform Act lays emphasis on the public availability of information as the key to raising attainment. That is where it most intimately affects teachers since they produce and use that information. The key to successful school management will be in reconciling professional concern with information on children learning with the new demands that this information be given to parents and made public at the school level. The initiatives that have changed education have come, and will continue to come, from teachers – through their concern with learning. If these initiatives are to continue they will require a management style aimed at encouraging teachers to go on being enterprising. Keeping staff informed will be the first priority.

All service organisations, including schools, depend on those involved knowing what is going on. Further, with a National Curriculum, locally financed and requiring collaboration between staff in a school, which also gives parents and pupils information at regular intervals, closing the classroom door and concentrating on your class or your subject is a disappearing option. So is the school that keeps its attainments to itself. The demand for information from both classroom and school has suddenly increased. More important, these two sets of information have been tied together.

Thus information is taken in this chapter as the key to the management of schools with learning as a priority. Many have of course flourished with most of the information in the minds of teachers not in filing cabinets. There it was available for use. Now the Education Act requires that much of that information is made public. It is seen as essential for parents as well as teachers. That is in line with the evidence in Chapters 5, 6 and 7. It could even up the life chances of children. The National Curriculum has not been applied to independent schools. Parents there know just what they want from such schools. So do most of their children. That is not the case in many maintained schools outside leafy suburbs in wealthy areas. Parents and pupils need to be informed. If maintained education is to flourish, responsibilities for learning must be shared. The provision of information is the first step in that sharing. This extends from marketing schools at one end to the confidential sharing of sensitive data between teacher and parent at the other. The concern is to ensure that information, which now has to be collected to meet the requirements of the 1988 Education Reform Act, is used to increase the effectiveness of learning.

Finally, the changes in the availability of information will, like all educational developments have unforeseen consequences. The packages of reforms introduced by the 1988 Education Reform Act and discussed in Chapter 2 have changed the direction in which information flows. Where administrative information flowed down and academic up, the Act increases the amount available and directs much of it outside as well as around the school. That circulation of information is more typical of modern, information-based organisations than of traditional top-down hierarchies. Management will have to be alert to the possibility that the Act will alter the structure of schools.

The uses of information

The importance of information can be seen in the extraordinary increase in the numbers earning their living by producing, processing and distributing it. IT, information technology, is the cutting edge of the sunrise industries. As those in manufacturing decrease, the number working with information has taken up the slack. Education itself is increasingly geared to produce those with the necessary skills. It is wise to be cautious about any possible 'revolution' in learning as a consequence. What is clear however is that we have at last appreciated that information is the key to successful management. Within organisations two uses of information can be separated. First, it enables management to control and to plan. Second, it can empower staff, putting them in a position to see what is needed and supporting them in taking the necessary action. That is the subject of Chapter 10.

Information for management

Controlling the organisation
All organisations depend on the availability of data enabling management to organise, monitor and adjust routines. In schools it is necessary to get the right teachers into the right rooms with the right children at the right time, with the right resources. It is particularly important in financial planning and will loom large in schools with local management. That is why LEAs will be working with schools to produce performance indicators. It is why schools will need to have accounting procedures. It is the substance of budgets, based on past activities and results and related to current activities and future targets. It is the subject of many books following the Education Act of 1988 (see for example Davies and Braund, 1989).

The impact of the 1988 Education Reform Act was summarised in Chapter 2 by pointing to three overlapping, interlocking packages.

Thus the information required to manage the school finances cannot be separated from the way schools are governed and the way learning is organised. The political point is clear in arrangements for local financial management. LEAs will take a strategic role, free from exercising detailed control over spending in schools. They will support governing bodies with professional advice. In law the governors control spending and therefore the appointment and dismissal of staff. The amount of information required in the school to control the budget will increase (see Coopers and Lybrand, 1988). Much of this will be used for monitoring by the LEA. That monitoring is supposed to ensure that local management is delivering better education. The information for controlling expenditure is supposed to give governors and LEA indications of costs related to their effectiveness in promoting learning. The need to control spending is going to have a direct and top-down impact on the way learning is organised.

There is also a new demand for control information directly related to learning. The LEA has the responsibility to ensure, through its inspectors, that the National Curriculum is being implemented in line with the Act and subsequent Orders. Regulations spell out the information that has to be produced in schools and made public. LEAs have established arrangements for dealing with complaints about the school curriculum. Parents will be able to use these local procedures if they are dissatisfied. Once again, this is threatening to teachers used to keeping much of their information of attainments private. The amount of information for control is being increased fast.

Planning the organisation

Planning in schools is complicated by the difficulties in decision-making outlined in Chapter 4. Ends and means tend to get confused. Yet the school effectiveness evidence confirms the importance of a headteacher who has clear goals for the school and who has managed to get staff to share in striving for them. The information required is usually long-term and in broader terms than control data. Many LEAs have encouraged schools to produce plans involving review and assessment, the specification of objectives and ways of reaching them. This is usually a 'systems' approach, very popular in the 1970s, based on the specification of goals and feedback from evaluations of the means introduced to achieve them. This approach has tended to go out of fashion in industry where the plans tended to inhibit responses to fast changing markets. But in education, such plans can indicate ways forward and keep teachers and the public involved with the school in the picture. It is easy to mock Management by Objectives or Programme Budgeting Systems. They did seem to be little concerned with learning and divorced from the political aspects of school life. But they did ensure that those involved knew what was supposed to be going on. Simplified and practical ways forward based on these are now available (see for example Caldwell and Spinks, 1988).

1 School review for planning

All teachers plan ways forward. This can consist of casual dis-cussion or thorough review. The years ahead have to be con-sidered, even if the decision has often been to carry on as before. But that option may now be suicidal. Even in the 1970s, with falling school rolls and talk of accountability it was risky. That was the time when school self-evaluation became popular. Like most innovations reported in Chapter 6, this movement lost its momentum. Yet it remains influential as schools try to work out their future post-1988.

The evaluation to serve as a basis for planning ahead has several labels such as school review, school self-evaluation and in-school evaluation. The common idea is that regular and systematic evalu-ations of ends and means is essential to identify strengths and weaknesses and to act to improve the standards attained. The movement to self-evaluation reached its peak around 1980. Like other innovations it was boosted by academics and adopted by enthusiastic schools. Over half the LEAs produced some docu-mented scheme. GRIDS (Guidelines for Review and Institutional Development in Schools), produced by the National Development Centre for School Management Training, received support in the *Better Schools* programme (DES, 1986). Yet by the mid-1980s the momentum was lost. Turner and Clift (1985), investigating the impact of one of the best-documented and best-known LEA schemes found that three years after publication less than half the teachers claimed to have read it or recall it. Little or nothing seemed to have changed. The innovation faded away like most curriculum developments in an earlier decade. But the idea of review and planning remains.

Some LEAs managed to merge self-evaluation into ongoing practice. Leeds developed a scheme of cooperative assessment that combined self-assessment by staff working with LEA advisors. Oxfordshire and Brent introduced mandatory schemes. The Inner London Education Authority introduced regular school reviews. The idea of systematically reviewing policies and practices can be found in many schools. Such reviews are always part of school management, however implicit or casual.

A weakness of most self-evaluation schemes was their denial that teachers could be held responsible for outputs. That view recurs in academic writing on self-evaluation which was critical of any attempt to assess what was learned and relate it to how schools were organised (see for example Becher *et al*, 1981). By the end of the 1980s with Attainment Targets, regular assessments and published school results the subject of statutory orders, this view that teachers were responsible for processes not outcomes looked as academic as its origins. Self-evaluation is too valuable to jettison with the literature that restricted it. It can be a way of relating school organisation to results and of checking whether the information being collected is being used effectively. The introduction of an assessment-led National Curriculum meant that school self-evaluation will be able to draw on output indicators, not only for each year group, but for the school as a whole. LEA and national comparisons will be possible. This is a technically dubious exercise, but it will be mandatory. Further, the 1988 Education Reform Act also increased the demand for data for accounting. Just as the Act produced a new data base on pupil attainments, so it demanded new indicators of school perform-ance. Across ten years the data for school review has multiplied (see for example Shipman, 1979).

2 *Planning at the classroom level*
At the centre of the information that can be used to promote learning is assessment. That serves many purposes. It is formative in providng feedback on how work is going, what is going right or wrong, where effort should be directed, how the curriculum might be changed. It is summative in showing attainment at the end of a course and providing grades for comparisons or selection,

or prediction. It also emphasises the priority of learning. If it is assesseed, it is important. Every teacher knows and uses assessment for these purposes every minute of the working day. Teaching is about assessment. Some small part is recorded. The extra effort required for this means that the information should be used to obtain maximum impact from the minimum effort.

The evidence on the curriculum and its evaluation, on curriculum change and the psychology of learning reported in Chapters 6 and 7 can be pulled together to guide management by the adoption of a simple model of the part played by assessment in the learning process. The evidence on the curriculum provides clues on the way changes can be made to stick. The evidence on learning gives guidance on practical steps that can improve learning. The common factor in practice is assessment. The learning situation can be modelled as follows.

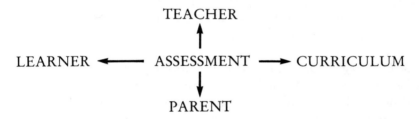

This diagram shows the central position of assessment. The information obtained informs the teacher who can then act to advise both pupil and parent, to adjust teaching style or the curriculum. It is central to matching the curriculum to the attainment of children, to sequencing work and giving it the right pace. Assessment is of course only one aspect of teaching. But it is through assessment that teachers act to support learning. It enables them to reinforce learning not only through words, but through signs, sighs and smiles. This is the most valuable kind of instantaneous feedback. Occasionally some of it is translated into comments, grades and marks on work. Some of this becomes formalised in tests and examinations, whether internal or external. Summaries are sent home to parents and discussed with children. This total body of assessment links the curriculum to the children, the learning tasks to the learner.

This view of assessment as central to learning has been reinforced by the introduction of a national curriculum. The prominent position for assessment was not new. The Better Schools policy had specified improved assessment as essential not only for pupil attainment and teacher performance, but that of the school itself (DES, 1985b). Teachers had anticipated this demand, particularly in the primary schools, where diagnostic assessment and screening had increased in popularity. Teachers had also worked with LEA advisors to produce curriculum guidelines and materials that contained means of assessment to help children as they learned. In secondary schools this was less apparent, yet in the years up to the introduction of GCSE, graded assessment had been the fastest growing area of public examination, largely because it provided formative information. In GCSE, coursework was providing feedback during rather than at the end of the courses. As the National Curriculum was introduced, guidelines for Records of Achievement were published, based on the same formative principle (DES, 1989). Formative assessment gives the information that can help learners, parents and teacher to appreciate strengths and weaknesses and work for improvement.

3 *Bringing school and classroom planning together*
In Chapter 1 the divide between management information flowing down and information on learning flowing up was identified as an unusual and unfortunate feature of schools. By the mid-1980s the gap was being pinpointed in analyses of the school curriculum (see for example DES, 1985a). Many children were either opting out of important subjects or not covering important areas within them. After 1988, teachers still have the responsibility for ensuring that their curriculum remains broad and balanced. The National Curriculum Council has the same responsibility at national level. The assessment of the National Curriculum is supposed to ensure that children's learning is sustained and encouraged by providing information on levels achieved on attainment targets, thus securing continuity and matching (DES, 1988).

This consideration of learning in relation to progression through the curriculum should not be buried in the effort to get the National Curriculum and its assessment in place. It is essential to keep learning up front. Planning can not mean unthinking implementation. The National Curriculum is defined through brief Attainment Targets and Programmes of Study. It provides a framework only. The breadth and balance of the curriculum and the progression of children through it still has to be secured by teachers. Much of the planning will have to be across the school. But it will depend on information gathered first in the classroom. To ensure that each child progresses as intended will take more than the mechanical implementation of assessment. It will be easy to tick statements of attainment achieved. The ten levels on each Attainment Target are very broad. It will be useful to have these levels defined. But the responsibility will still lie with teachers to ensure that the entitlement to a broad and balanced education is secured for individual children.

The mandatory provision of information on learning is then a burden but also an opportunity for teachers. It is a challenge to school management to use it effectively. The 1988 Education Reform Act will take a decade to implement. Even then it will need continual development, partly to rectify early mistakes, partly to respond to further social and economic change. The flood of publications will continue. It will be essential to organise the collection and distribution of this material so that all teachers and as many governors and parents as possible know what is being proposed or imposed. Combined with information on attainments it can share responsibilities for learning. Too many children and parents have drifted along without much idea of what's going on.

The worst scenario would be for the effort to produce this information to be wasted by leaving the data in files. It would be equally wasteful to contain it within the school. Once the assessment of the National Curriculum is in place, teachers will be tracking children up ten levels on around fifty attainment targets. They will report summaries of this progress at the four reporting ages of 7, 11, 14 and 16. In between, the progress charted on each child can be used, not only by the teacher to help the child, but to involve the parents. They have a statutory right to receive information at the end of the four key stages. They will discuss this with teachers. That is a short step from encouraging them to see and discuss the detailed progress sheets on which the reporting at the end of key stages is based. This promises a wealth of information as a base for cooperation over learning between teacher, child and parent.

It is of course easy to ignore the technical problems in getting National Curriculum assessment into a valid and reliable form. It is an extraordinarily ambitious and technically difficult development. In the end it has to rely on teacher judgements, even if these can be guided by Standard Assessment Tasks, by in-service training and moderation meetings. The assessment tail is tending to wag the curriculum dog. Yet it is an opportunity to move beyond using assessment for planning and for control to increased empowerment and a spread of responsibility. That is the subject of Chapter 10.

Mining the data

The increase in available data as the Education Act is implemented means that there is more available to use to answer questions about children learning. Unfortunately there is less time to dig it out. Some will have to be produced for LEAs. But as the National Curriculum assessments are implemented it will not be difficult to answer some important questions about the success of the school in securing the 'entitlement' that is the justification of the National Curriculum. For example, each of the following issues could be illuminated by the tabulation of data that will have to be stored for reporting purposes.

1   The levels achieved in specific subjects by girls and boys as they progress through school.

2   The progress made by children from different social class or ethnic group.

3   The impact of identifiable teaching styles, curriculum innovations, ways of involving parents, of managing the school.

4   The resources allocated to children with special educational needs and their attainments.

Rightly, it can be objected that the indicators are crude. But teachers are going to be asked questions about such issues as parents receive more information, not only on their own children, but on the performance of the school. The school results will have to be put into a context. Mining the available data helps. Over the years, time series which show changes year by year, make the data more meaningful.

Organising and reviewing the information

The collection, updating and use of information cannot be exempt from scrutiny for cost. Most headteachers take responsibility for the collection and distribution of information. That is unlikely to be possible in the future, particularly when there will be demands for financial as well as administrative and academic information. The easiest task to delegate is the collection and distribution of externally produced documents. Somebody on the staff should build up an archive of recent information on the implementation of the Education Act of 1988, for use by staff, governors and parents. It will involve keeping an eye on the educational press and sending for new publications as they appear.

The most difficult task is to coordinate the new information requirements with those already in existence. The Education Act has increased the amount of information required from schools. This cannot be added to that already collected without some streamlining. Hence there are several steps in the necessary reorganisation. Every school has some arrangement for collecting and distributing information on the curriculum and the achievements of pupils. That working data is stored in classrooms, departments and headteacher's office. There is rarely any discussion of it as a whole. Some of it is duplicated. Some of it is collected more than once. Some of it is never used, once collected. As new demands build up it is essential to review what is collected. Demands from LEA for monitoring, from examination boards, from headteachers, for the production of records of achievement, for reports to parents, to careers service, references for employers, transfer information for receiving schools, for HMI and researchers need to be met, but as far as possible from data collected to meet the demands of the National Curriculum and for recording. Behind the necessary review must lie the reconciliation of management information with information on learning. That is why the whole staff have to be convinced of the need to review. Some information is jealously guarded as a source of power. Headteachers as well as those in classrooms may have to give more if the collection of information is to be made cost-effective.

Informing and marketing

The Education Act of 1980 required schools to provide brochures for parents. The Act also allowed freer movement of pupils across LEA boundaries. The 1988 Act pushed both of these further and by introducing open enrolment reinforced the idea that schools should engage in marketing (see for example Brunt, 1987). The danger in this move is to think that image can be divorced from reality. For all the hype involved, marketing of schools depends on the real, not the displayed quality, on the clarity of school aims and the effectiveness of teaching. Cosmetics are likely to be superficially attractive. As stressed in Chapter 1, schools are not comfortable around the leading edge of change. Further, education is a service industry and the staff tend to be part of the product. Parents buy a school because they think the teachers are good. Hence, even with national assessments, it is likely that the success of a school will be in the way staff present rather than sell themselves and the school. Thus the marketing strategy for schools has to be to get all staff to accept their individual responsibility for the school as a whole.

Four key factors are usually stressed in marketing strategy, product, place, price and promotion. For service industries such as education, a fifth P, people, is usually added. The 1988 Education Reform Act forces schools to produce and publish more information on product, to put it into a context which includes place or catchment area and gives teachers local control over the costs of organising a school in a particular way. The Act also makes it more important to be sensitive to customer, parent and pupil satisfaction. Waiting and using loss of intake as an indicator of loss of public confidence reduces the time to take remedial action and makes it likely that this will have to be done with reduced resources as these are tied to school roll. This points to the importance not of marketing but of sensitivity to parents and public. The school that listens will do better than one that preaches.

Two marketing questions need to be asked in all schools.
1 *Is there a distinctive and public image of the school?*
This is not just the consequence of schools being placed in the market by open enrolment. It is the basis for knowing where the

school is supposed to be going. It accounts for the emphasis on effective schools having a distinctive ethos, climate, feel. That is also why the image has to be visible to parents. If they are to help their children they need to know what the school is doing. So do employers.

The introduction of records of achievement is an example. A major problem was convincing employers that positive statements would give them sufficient information. The solution, as with other recent developments such as GCSE, TVEI, curriculum developments in primary schools and the National Curriculum itself, is to secure support through publicising what the school stands for and the place of records. Employers will have confidence in positive statements if they trust the school. This issue of public image is now discussed as marketing. But it is more than that. It is a way of securing the support of those who are important influences on the motivation of children to learn.

2 Are all teachers involved in establishing and supporting the image?
In Chapter 1 a distinctive characteristic of schools was shown to be the frequency with which individually successful teachers could remain detached from the running of the school. Collegiality, now seen as an important feature, particularly in primary and middle schools (see Campbell, 1985), often excludes colleagues who have only a marginal interest in the way the school is managed. The bounded rationality discussed in Chapter 1 is often the result of teachers not knowing and not wanting to know what the school stands for. They can still be excellent at their job. But they don't work as part of the team. As discussed in Chapter 2, that situation is perilous given the power of parents and governors following 1988. However effective, teachers who remain detached are increasingly likely to block the flow of information now required to manage the school and meet the external demands.

10 The management of learning: empowering the staff

You have to be an optimist to write about teachers taking initiatives as they suffer under badly-thought-out legislation and rushed implementation. Yet the evidence in Chapter 4 points to the continuing ability of teachers to move the service in the direction dictated by their experience with children in the classroom. That does not mean that the 1988 Act will not radically change the educational scene. It does mean that nobody can predict what that scene will look like in the year 2000. Across the last decade of the century the efforts of teachers in their classrooms will continue to adapt the way learning is organised. Education was described in Chapter 4 as a minefield of unintended consequences. But these are also the intended consequences of the convictions and actions of thousands of teachers. It is the intentions of policy-makers that do not work out. The 1988 Act assumes that this local development will continue. That is why it is important to look for a management training and a management style in schools that will energise teachers rather than constrain them. That is the subject of this chapter. Because it looks ahead, it also changes gear, shifting to prescription.

The current state of staff development

The emphasis on staff development in school management training is justified because it is nearly half a million teachers who really determine the success or failure of education. Part of that training has been devoted to preparing teachers for promotion, particularly to headship. There has also been in-service training for head-teachers. There are three serious gaps. First, there is no career planning stretching from initial training, through induction to posts of responsibility. It is too easy for teachers to remain on the margin of developments, possibly effective in the classroom, but not engaged beyond it. Second, staff development is rarely treated in in-service courses as a way of stimulating initiative. Third, these courses tend to be divorced from direct concern with learning. Staff development has the same constraining approach as the rest of school management training.

The absence of career development in teaching arises partly from the odd status of teachers. In England and Wales they are public but not civil servants. They are paid by LEAs, not central government. Unlike most countries where they are paid by central government, they can go to any LEA that will appoint them without direction by central government to shortage areas. Their training is a direct concern of central government who determine teacher training numbers and lay down minimum conditions for the accreditation of institutions for teacher education. These include the hours for work on academic subjects, on courses in the teaching of core subjects and on teaching practice. The staff of training institutions have also to return periodically to the classroom if they are engaged on professional work. This regulation has been increased across the 1980s. Yet once a first post is obtained by the newly-qualified, it can be the end of formal career development.

The probationary year may consist of just a visit by an inspector to confirm that there is no disaster and occasionally attendance at a course organised by the employing LEA. Once qualified teacher status is obtained, obligations to engage in further training cease. It is rare to find any sustained induction arrangements in schools. Staff development is rightly a priority in in-service training. Even then, it may only attract the ambitious and the interested, who are often the least in need of it.

The importance of staff development arises from its position as a link between top-down and bottom-up developments. It is not just that any legislation involving curriculum and management depends on teachers for implementation. It is the teachers who link management to learning, who develop the latter and keep education up-to-date. As the social changes described in Chapter 3 continue, teachers will be adjusting education to their new customers in their new social conditions. The 1988 Education Reform Act will affect this by giving parents more information and more access to the information held in the school. This may not always be welcome, but it should make teachers more aware of the changing demands of parents and the reasons for the changing behaviour of pupils. So should in-service training as it relates developments imposed by legislation to practices in the schools.

The various titles of books and courses on staff development suggest that they are however little concerned with learning. That arises because many of them are preparing teachers for promotion, often out of the classroom. These courses also tend to adopt a top-down approach. The term 'staff development' itself suggests processing for future roles rather than encouragement to continue with efforts to improve the management of learning. The academic titles are even more forbidding. 'Human resource development' and 'human resource management' suggest constraint. The intention is to improve the effectiveness of management. The emphasis is on developing potential, but without reference to learning and by recommending procedures that restrict the scope to innovate. The changes in the funding of in-service training have reinforced this constraining approach. The academic courses that were the victims of the new arrangements were sometimes designed to promote detached and critical perspectives on existing practice. Their contraction, in pre- as well as in-service training, would be acceptable if substituted by others helping teachers to stand back and review practice. But many were designed to promote established procedures and few were directly concerned with learning.

The low priority for staff development concerned with improving learning can be seen from lists of topics used to organise in-service courses. Personnel management, staff selection, staff appraisal, conditions of service, disciplinary procedures and grievance procedures are popular subjects. The concern is with evaluation and appraisal, counselling, conflict resolution, managing emotional issues, stress and change, personal motivation. There are many courses designed to get teachers to reflect on practice and work out ways forward in the classroom. But the tendency is to see staff development as a management tool for convergence, rather than as a way of promoting divergent enterprise aimed at raising attainment.

There is also a difficulty in the priorities for staff development as the demands made on in-service training increase. The National Curriculum is unbalancing the staffing of schools as Orders are made for core and foundation subjects. In primary schools many staff will find it hard to cope with compulsory science and technology. Many are too small to have postholders or others who can advise, even in a core subject such as mathematics. In-service training is going to be necessary for using Standard Assessment Tasks, combining results from these with teacher assessments and moderating the final levels given to pupils at meetings with colleagues. This has added to the demand just as many areas have run into a teacher shortage. There is little room left for courses that are not concerned with immediate crises.

The solution for staff development must then lie largely outside in-sevice training and in the management of schools. If teachers are to be encouraged to follow appropriate career paths and fulfil potential that will have to be done through the roles they play as part of their job. The focus of the rest of this chapter is therefore on the potential for school management to promote development and particularly initiative among staff.

The effective school stretches staff by sharing responsibilities. That applies to new as well as established teachers. Indeed, induction, the first step on the career path, is best organised through a programme that steadily increases responsibilities in line with growing confidence. The suggestions that follow are prescriptive but based on the evidence presented earlier. In Chapter 11 these prescriptions for empowerment will be related to developments in the management of modern industries.

From staff development to empowerment

Those who are starved of information have to accept what is going on or blindly reject it. Knowledge is power. The school effectiveness evidence reported in Chapter 5 suggests that an important influence on attainment in schools is the involvement of staff in decision-making, in establishing high expectations and in taking initiatives. That comes from a particular style of leadership and management. It involves the following aspects.

1 *Planning careers*
The danger in teaching is in getting stuck in mid-career. These teachers are often effective, but talent is wasted. School

management should include career planning for all staff, starting with the recruits. This will involve regular discussion of aspirations and opportunities for meeting them. It will involve obtaining information about appropriate further training. Often it will mean obtaining advice from inspectors or advisors. Regular teacher appraisal will help establish this planning and should give it priority. But the key remains the regular discussion of prospects and performance, opportunities and training needs.

2 *Regular appraisal*

Many schools now have schemes of teacher appraisal. The government has been supporting pilot projects with Education Support Grants. It forms a central part in planning careers and increasing job satisfaction. For a minority of teachers it is a threat. Teaching can be a misery as well as a joy. The closed classroom door can not only block the flow of information for management, but conceal jubilation and tribulation. The task of management is to provide support and encourage learning in the job. As with all learning, that means the provision of regular and quick feedback, particularly when something goes well. Teacher appraisal is only the formal part of a supportive management. There will be hopeless cases. Local financial management and open enrolment are now combined to make these more difficult. Inevitably appraisal during the probationary year will have to be given priority. But it should be a support for teachers at all stages of their careers.

3 *Job enrichment*

The more depressed teachers become through imposed constraints, the more important it is to provide rewards within the school. This is reflected in the importance of culture in school effectiveness studies. In some schools teachers feel appreciated. In others they feel unsupported. In the former they are involved in decision-making, are consulted, are given responsibilities. They do their job in the classroom but share in the excitement of collaborating with colleagues in moving the school forward. They feel that their problems are shared and their successes rewarded.

4 *Delegation for development*

Delegation will be essential as the burdens on senior staff increase following the 1988 Education Reform Act. But delegation should not be a way of shuffling off unwanted tasks. It is an effective form of career development. It is a way of giving staff responsibilities, enabling them to take initiatives and adding to the views on how to move forward. Even the most junior staff have strengths that can be used. Some tasks are ideal for those at the start of their career or on an academic course. For example, the collection and distribution of information on the implementation of the 1988 Act will be useful for staff, personally rewarding and bring the teacher into contact with governors and, occasionally, interested parents.

5 *A clear communication policy*
Staff in effective schools know where it is supposed to be going, what it stands for and the role they are supposed to play. Information is shared by planning its circulation. It is two-way so that management receives information as well as gives it. In that way headteacher and senior staff not only know how their actions are being received, know whether the messages from them are getting through, but benefit from the views of others. Staff are encouraged to share their particular interests whether from courses being attended or activity in the community or knowledge of developments elsewhere. Above all, it is a policy, agreed by senior staff, aiming to keep staff informed, working as a team and participating.

6 *Receptiveness to new ideas*
The advantage of perambulating headteachers is that they can ask for and listen to the ideas of staff. These can be bounced off other staff later in the walk. This can be extended to inviting solutions to problems that are emerging. Few staff meetings are prepared with this as a technique, but inviting suggestions in advance for meeting specific problems can involve even junior staff. Many schools use brainstorming techniques during in-service days for the same purpose. Others use the working party. The techniques are less important than the attitudes. Ideas are too important to be immediately rejected. They should always be acknowledged, slept on and receive a response. Teachers in the classroom are often in the best position to keep the management focused on learning.

These six prescriptions are ways of developing staff through their work. They are more likely to be effective than in-service courses because the learning is continuous and on-the-job. They mean that school management has to take these development responsibilities seriously. It also means that management has to be prepared to listen. Above all it means that the culture of learning that lies behind school effectiveness, applies to and affects staff as well as pupils. It is easy to laugh at books entitled The Learning School, The Self-Evaluating School or The Self-Managing School (see for example Caldwell and Spinks, 1985), but they are spelling out an important point. The effective school develops staff as well as pupils.

The extension of empowerment: motivating pupils

The payoff from empowerment lies behind the moves to involve pupils in their own learning. Negotiations, contracts, target-setting are all symptoms of a move to giving more responsibility to learners. Schools involved in pilot studies for Records of Achievement were particularly excited by the motivation generated by the discussions that formed part of formative recording (DES, 1989a). It was time-consuming. The pilot work started at 14 when this negotiation was difficult for pupils coming to it for the first time. But it showed the teachers involved how valuable it was to face pupils with decisions about their progress, what they could achieve and what should be recorded as important. In the compact organised by the Inner London Education Authority there were some 1500 school leavers provided with jobs by 1989. They achieved this after fulfilling the targets for attendance, punctuality, homework deadlines, public examinations agreed with employers. These were usually under-motivated young people responding to the challenge of responsibility.

In many primary schools, staff would wonder what the fuss was about. Young children are often given responsibility for setting their own targets and discussing the extent to which they have been achieved. The same surprise would be felt in many secondary schools involved in Technical and Vocational Education, the Lower Achieving Pupils Project and with developed Personal and Social Education courses. These share an approach through giving responsibility to the learner. The expanding role of coursework in GCSE is a move in the same direction. Just as staff development is best achieved on the job by allocating responsibilities, so progress is often best achieved by pupils sharing in the setting of targets and the evaluation of results.

The extension of empowerment: involving parents

The 1988 Act makes parents partners sharing information that used to be the property of teachers. The frequency of reporting is to be increased. At the four reporting ages for National Curriculum assessments parents will receive profiled information on the attainment of their children. They will discuss this with teachers. In between the reporting ages they will be able to discuss progress on attainment targets. Records of achievement will give them detail 'across and beyond' the National Curriculum.

This extension is in line with local developments, particularly in primary schools, in the teaching of reading and mathematics. The former is sufficiently established to be known by the initials PITR, parental involvement in the teaching of reading. This has arisen from both theoretical and practical advances in knowledge about how children learn. First, children are seen to learn through their total experience, not just through what is presented in school. Second, the evidence on the advantages of learning at home in a one-to-one, warm situation have been appreciated (see for example Tizard and Hughes, 1984).

The movement has gone furthest in the teaching of reading (see for example Topping and Wolfendale, 1985). While the evidence suggests that there is no certain improvement from such schemes, they have been expanded rapidly. Their importance is as much in involving parents as in the gains in reading. The schemes have been used with poor and rich, with those whose first language is not English, in most regions of the country. They are a symptom of a move to making parents welcome in education. The combination of increased information and involvement will give a powerful message to parents that they have a part to play that is active, not passive.

The extension of empowerment: responsibilities

It has been stressed that rights and duties go together. Empowering teachers, pupils and parents will mean new definitions of the part each is expected to play. For teachers it will mean giving up some professional authority. The informed parent cannot be fobbed off when they press to see the performance of their child against Attainment Targets. But these parents should have learned that the acknowledgement of their importance in learning and of their involvement in it means that they cannot place responsibility solely on the teacher. The result is likely to be more open, honest education. With the social changes detailed in Chapter 3 this should be an opportunity for raising attainment by securing support from the home.

The responsibilities of pupils have already been discussed. They too will have to accept that learning is their business. This is optimistic, but the combination of school and home is powerful. Employers are increasingly willing to play their part in producing contracts and using records of achievement that contain statements negotiated between pupil and teacher. Once again the clue lies in the culture for learning. Schools cannot do the job against the antagonism of the community. That situation has resulted in gross inequalities in attainment between schools for rich and poor. Sharing responsibilities will not close that gap, but would bring a greater number of the population into a position where home reinforces school. The way forward has to be to work for cooperation. So far rights have been given preference over responsibilities. That is unfair on teachers. They take the blame for situations over which they may have little influence. Education needs to be moved in a contractual direction. That is an important task for school management. The political package is now in place giving governors and parents extra rights. Schools need to be managed to press home the message that this also carries responsibilities.

Providing the incentives for enterprise

So far job enrichment has been discussed within the context of the school. But an education service that expects teachers to continue to play an active part in further development also needs to provide incentives. It is unlikely that these will come through raised salaries. It is likely that the burden of implementing current legislation will increase. Teacher morale is low because the changes demanded are not only extensive, but unclear in their detail. Many are threatened by an imposed change in the curriculum leaving their expertise unwanted. It is an unpromising scenario for the advent of the enterprise culture.

To establish incentives for enterprise is not however an uphill task. Teachers have shown remarkable initiative in adjusting education right where it matters, with the children, as they learn. That will continue because it is there that the motivation lies. A glance at the reports of new developments in the Times Educational Supplement each week confirms this vitality. Thus the incentives would be rewarding initiative where it is already most lively. Here are a few suggestions.

1 *Central government could*

- allocate part of the Educational Support Grant budget to enable teachers to develop and extend promising innovations already in place and confirmed as successful by HMI or LEA inspectors.
- establish a small grants budget to support teachers taking initiatives. This will be particularly valuable once local financial management limits the capacity of LEAs to help.
- establish an Educational Honours list giving public recognition for outstanding service.

2 *Local Education Authorities could*

- establish information exchange schemes on the lines of the Inner London Education Authority's INDEX scheme. This would provide an outlet for good ideas and inform others of them.
- set up initiatives funds to reward teachers who produce ideas that will help other schools.
- network teachers working on common developments to advise the authority and neighbouring schools.

3 *Governors and parents could*
- establish their own fund for teacher initiatives, particularly in the area of home-school relations.
- take the initiative in mobilising support for the school, particularly in involving minority communities, local people with particular skills and local employers. The Industrial Fund example in Chapter 6 was ambitious, but many schools now benefit from such support.

- liaise with voluntary organisations to ensure that schools in poor areas are not left unsupported.

4 *Headteachers could*
- establish project teams that cut across departments or year groups to work on longer-term developments, using junior staff as coordinators.
- establish action learning teams wherein each member can raise their own issues for the rest to work on and resolve.
- use the opportunities of local financial management to reserve funds for new developments, using this reserve as a means of staff development.

These ideas may seem daft to harassed teachers struggling with new Attainment Targets, Programmes of Study and Standard Assessment Tasks. But they are all aimed at promoting bottom-up development. We may deserve a teaching force that concentrates on the National Curriculum and religious education and sticks to the conditions on professional duties specified by government (DES, 1987). But that is not how the service has been developed or is planned to develop. While responsibility for the future lies with teachers they need to be encouraged to work towards it. The most effective staff development I have ever experienced has been where teachers were entrusted with the task of developing a record of achievement scheme for a group of LEAs. The task was accomplished cost-effectively, was based on an intimate knowledge of the conditions in the trial schools, kept to schedule and consequently delivered the system required. We have a teaching force that accepts its role in moving the service forward. Seeing the benefit for children is often sufficient reward in itself.

Will the new information flow change the school organisation?

This may seem an academic question following a polemic on the conditions for enterprise. Yet it is an appropriate way to end these chapters on information. The current changes in the quantity and quality of information is important enough to alter the way schools will be run. Information has to be managed. Its importance in empowering staff, in motivating pupils and involving parents suggests however that it is not passive. It is an influence on the shape of the organisation itself. The monitorial school with pupil-teacher ratios of over a hundred to one, with often unwilling children and resentful parents, kept the former under strict control and the latter at a distance. These schools were rigidly hierarchical. The teacher set the tasks. The pupil teachers and monitors relayed it to the pupils. They signalled when it was complete. The next task was set. The teacher's pay was often settled by the measured successes of the pupils in the three Rs by a visiting inspector. It was a mechanical system with top-down communication and an authoritative headteacher.

Across a century schools have become more relaxed and democratic, particularly with teachers who are now professionally trained before entry. Yet most retain a hierarchical structure. Will the new flow of information restructure the school? The issue is neatly raised by Drucker (1986). Most traditional organisations are hierarchical, based originally on the military. Indeed, in many countries the army remains the only efficient bureaucracy. Hence the popularity of military dictatorships. These organisations work by having clear chains of command. At each level information is received, sorted out and passed on, selectively to the next rank down. At the bottom you go over the top not knowing why.

Modern organisations with advanced information technology have no need for a hierarchy to handle information. Middle management is being slimmed down. At all levels information is accessible through a terminal or printout. Drucker suggests that the model now is a symphony orchestra. Players and conductor have the score. They all know what is going on. The 1988 Education Reform Act is making schools produce more information and to circulate it, internally and externally. It may change schools in the symphonic direction. It is an exciting prospect. The headteacher as conductor can display all the talents of the virtuoso. But all the orchestra have to play their part. One false note can spoil the performance, put off the customers. The real skill of the conductor is to make even the back row of the violins know that it all depends on them. Such an organisation is disciplined. There will be losses. Generals do not readily give up command. The control of information in schools as elsewhere consolidates control at the top. Once it is shared, authority is harder to maintain. It will be interesting to see if the metaphors of schooling change in this directon. What is certain is that information has to be on the training agenda. It links school management to learning.

11 Management and the search for excellence

In this Chapter the focus is on attempts to understand and improve school management. All share a remarkable inconsistency. It means that caution has to be exercised. Recommendations are influenced by the political as well as the theoretical stance of the author, by the times and the prevailing conditions, as well as the evidence available. A reliable guide is that any course, book or article has taken about a year to produce and has probably been overtaken by events. Books and courses are only slowly revised. Recommendations from experience also contradict and go out of date. Whether the approach is from theory or from practice there is unlikely to be consistency.

F. W. Taylor published *Scientific Management* in 1911 after years of carefully observing the way men shovelled and heaved. The results of this observation was a scientific management to produce the maximum output at minimum cost. We have moved a long way from this world of heavy manual labour, but this classical theory of administration, remains important. We still search for efficiency and still reward to sustain effort. We still use terms like cost-effective, reinforcement and piece-work. There is always an emphasis on productivity in management.

By the 1930s an alternative, contrasting theory of management emphasising human relations was in vogue. Significantly the pioneering research was in lighter assembly work in the Western Electric Company in Chicago (Roethlisberger and Dickson, 1939). Now the stress was on the importance of relations within groups, of productivity as a response to respect and information rather than money. The terms in use now included belonging, knowing and trust.

These two management approaches remain important. 'Speedy' Taylor is a rather derided figure, but his stress on the connection between pay and effort remains important. Indeed, for all the attraction of the human relations school of management, it can substitute a warm climate for a decent wage. The structure that Taylor emphasised and the culture that lies at the heart of human relations can be found at the centre of books and courses today. For fifty years the pendulum has swung. The Education Reform Act of 1988 is likely to swing the emphasis for schools back to structure defined by assessment targets and performance indicators. But the pendulum won't stop there,. Management has to operate in changing environments, and the search for success swings attention from structure to culture despite the obvious link between them.

These polar positions are a clue to cutting through the jungle of management theories. Advocates press their case hard and each contains some truth. But no simple theory fits the complexity of all organisations or all changes in their contexts. The poles and all the intermediate positions do however yield an *aide-memoire* of points to look at as you manage. Throughout this chapter there are contrasts and contradictions as the evidence is examined. This may be alarming. Don't panic. There's less in this than meets the eye! Somewhere between structure and culture, between centralisation and decentralisation, between formal and informal, between detailed planning and intuition, between managing for comfort and for performance, most teachers will find a position that suits.

Three approaches to management

Three ways of viewing and recommending management approaches will be considered here. The first two, incrementalism and modelling, are included because they are met in the literature on management and lie behind many books and courses on school management. The third, the search for excellence, is given more space because it has been very influential in education and approaches evidence in the same way as HMI and educational researchers looking at school effectiveness. All three approaches are based on evidence collected by observation or survey. But the evidence is used very differently.

The incremental approach: why are practical tips so unconvincing?

The incremental approach to management is familiar throughout the education service. Each year the DES, the LEAs and the schools use it to decide on the allocation of resources. This is not usually preceded by any extensive review of policies and practices, but by adding on a bit here and taking off a bit there from what has been done in the past. Managers start with an existing organisation running in an established way. Changes are usually made by adjusting round the edges rather than radical revision at the centre. It was argued in Chapter 2 that the 1988 Education Reform Act has changed the way schooling is packaged and that this requires major changes in management. But no headteacher or staff, or governor can start afresh. Teachers are in post and procedures are set. Further, in schools stability is necessary for learning to be effective.

It is in this incremental way that teachers and others settle into established ways of working that inhibit radical change by management. But it also suggests that the consequent incrementalism is not just expedient. As decisions are made there is a history of events in the minds of those involved. Often there is an image of how the school, or the class, or the individual learner works best. It may be implicit, rarely explained, never formulated in a systematic way, but it acts as a reference for decisions, as a way of understanding. Indeed, such implicit images of how things work are behind most actions. From scientists setting out to examine a hypothesis derived from a developed model in their discipline to a child deciding whether to risk throwing a note across the room to a friend, there is some model of the situation and consequently some expectation of expected outcomes. 'Tips for teachers' actually contain implicit models of the school.

The incremental view is most frequently seen in books and on courses giving nuts and bolts advice on specific issues. Most hints are from experienced teachers, often with experience in pilot projects introducing the new arrangements. These practical tips are essential for teachers trying to implement new ways of doing old jobs. They are very popular and the funding of INSET has been changed to limit the scope of higher education to offer theoretical, academic courses. The problem with this lies in the implicit nature of the models used rather than in the absence of a model. Reading a book, listening to how to locally manage a school, how to work with governors, how to maintain discipline, how to develop staff and so on means putting the recommendations into context, into some implicit model of how a school works. But that model will not be the one used by the author or speaker. The recommendation will take on a different meaning implemented in a new context. The problem lies in the private nature of the models used by giver and taker.

The modelling approach: why is there so much disagreement?

The existence of implicit models behind incrementalism and the importance in management training of bringing these into the open links practical, tips-for-teachers approaches into those involving the consideration of established models. These are constructed to promote understanding. Every teacher models situations to deal with them. We have metaphors that help. This teacher sees a school class as a family. That teacher likes to see the class working like clockwork. The head sees the school as a haven in a troubled world wherein children develop naturally. The metaphor is used to describe the class or the school. But it is more than description. The image of family or clockwork or haven helps to explain how things seem to work. There is misunderstanding because each metaphor leads to different interpretations of the same events.

Morgan (1986) sees this reference to metaphors as fundamental to the management of organisations. Issues are thought through 'as if' the organisation was a building needing support, shoring up, demolishing, cleansing or falling apart. We imagine the school as a battleground needing a plan of attack, fall-back positions and reserves. To understand the organisation it is 'imaged' by using one or more metaphors. Indeed, Morgan recommends using a series of metaphors to get more than one view of how things are working out.

The favourite metaphors among teachers stress either structure or culture just as in management theory. On one side are machine metaphors. The school is seen as ticking over, as a system. The parts connect. You get things moving when the bell goes. You oil the works, give it a boost and keep up the momentum. When things run down you press the accelerator. When they get out of control you put your foot on the brake. The school is planned. There are objectives to be met, a timetable for meeting them, evaluation to check that there are no bugs in the engine and feed-back of information to monitor events. The management style here is likely to stress structures.

The other much-used metaphor is organic. The school is seen as an organism, a body, living, growing, flourishing, decaying. Now the parts are more than a system. They have some underlying unity. They perform functions for the working of the whole. It has an ethos and we talk as if it, rather than the individuals who serve in it, made decisions, faced crises and developed. This school is loved or hated. The children grow, are nurtured and mourn when they leave. We are firmly in the land of culture, where values not structure, belonging not organisation, are paramount.

Metaphors merge into models. The purpose of both is the same. They can be sources for understanding what is going on. But the model is usually built on observation or survey and opened to criticism to test its validity. It is a source of hypotheses and their investigation leads to elaborating the model. There are numerous ways of categorising the many models of schools that exist. The variety follows from the way models are constucted. Social scien-tists trying to understand how schools work draw on the theories in their discipline. This Marxist political scientist sees schools as servants of capitalism aiding the subjugation of the working class. That old sociologist sees the school in organic terms, evolving naturally, so it plays its part in socialising the young. This young social scientist sees schools in terms of the meanings that the people in them give to their situation. This is confusing, but each has the same purpose. The modelling is to promote understanding.

Events can be referred to the models as they can to the meta-phor, for interpretation. But now there is a constructed body of theory and evidence to aid that understanding or to start enquiries that will lead to confirming or refuting evidence. The models, unlike the metaphors, are laid out for public scrutiny and criticism.

Bush (1986) distinguishes five sets of models of the school. These are

> 1 formal models such as bureaucracy, where the organ-isation is treated as a rational hierarchical system. An example is Musgrove, (1971)

2   democratic models stressing collegiality, shared decision-making. An example is Campell (1985)

3   Political models, where the emphasis is on bargaining, conflict, negotiation. An example is Ozga, (1988)

4   subjective models focused on the way situations are defined, negotiated and given meaning. An example is Best (1983)

5   ambiguity models, including loose-coupled and garbage can versions where there is no apparent relation between ends and means. An example is Bell (1980).

Once again, teachers will recognise aspects of many of these models in their schools. None are 'correct', Each focuses attention on particular issues and procedures. At the same time as models yield ideas on how things work, they shut off other, alternative, ideas. Anyone devoted to one model will reject explanations that do not fit. That is why Marxists and so on are difficult to convince. Yet management models are not theories that can be proved wrong. They are beyond refutation. Hence they should be handled with care and the use of more than one is a safeguard against over-confidence.

To illustrate the use of such models we will return to the systems version of the formal models. This has been very influential. It is, for example, the model used by the National Development Centre for School Management Training (NDC), established at the University of Bristol in the 1980s to develop management training for schools (McMahon and Bolam, 1987). The sequence of events for LEA or school review starts with the specification of aims, proceeds to reviewing roles, policies and practices, goes on to establishing priorities, putting them into action and ends with an overview and plans for another round.

Yet the promise of these cycles of continual improvement has not been fulfilled. This results partly from the restrictions involved in a system model. The limitations of rational, linear decision-making were spelled out in Chapter 4. The assumption that schools are best modelled as systematic deflects attention from conflicts, from power, even from collegial, democratic debate. The model also tends to see the school as internally cohesive, thus ignoring the influence of parents and community. That was unfortunate just as education was being opened up to consumer influence.

The list of models above is not exhaustive. Further, ambiguity models do not really fit, for they are a denial of the possibility of building a model. The term 'loose-coupled' is often used here, implying that parts often work without reference to other parts or the whole. Staff work without apparent cohesion. The term 'garbage can' is also applied, again suggesting that a school in this category could not be modelled even if it would be a good subject for a novel. None of these models is a complete picture of reality, assembled from survey and observation, and tested and proven against reality. Any teacher can find many instances that do not fit any model. Authors may sound convincing, may believe that the school is part of the ideological apparatus of the capitalist state or a bureaucracy imposed on the population, or a group of colleagues reaching professional decisions, but exceptions abound. They should. Each model is just that, a synthetic construction to help understanding.

With this view of models as reference points, as sources of hunches about the way things work, their use in management is likely to be the same as for metaphors. Most of us switch models in search of hunches about the way things work. This increases our chance of insight. It is a useful approach for managers, acting as an improved *aide-memoire*. It suggests how decisions may affect the school and it informs choices by yielding different possible scenarios. Models are useful abstractions not pictures of reality. Their strength is their published, public nature. They alert listener and reader to the interpretations of the author.

The search for excellence: why are today's whizz-kids tomorrow's bankrupts?

There is an approach to management that is practical and similar to that of HMI and educational researchers as they look at schools. This starts by identifying successful organisations and ends with lists of the features that they share and which seem to account for their success. This is pragmatic, identifying what works. HMI have been doing it for over a century. It remains popular in industry and has been very influential in writing about education.

The most influential study was *In Search of Excellence* (Peters and Waterman, 1982). Both writers have remained active since then, writing independently (see for example, Peters, 1985 and 1988 and Waterman, 1988). *In Search of Excellence* sparked off other studies in the UK as well as the USA using the same method of looking at the management features of successful firms (see for example Goldsmith and Clutterbuck, 1984 for a British example and Clifford and Cavanagh, 1985 for an American example). The spin-off in education in Britain came in *Taken for Granted* (Handy, 1984). Handy, a professor in a business school, translated the factors identified by Peters and Waterman for American business firms into features found in effective schools. He also showed the similarity with the HMI study *Ten Good Schools* (DES, 1977).

Caution is needed about this approach to good management. Many of the factors are very difficult to apply to schools for reasons spelled out in Chapter 1. Firms identified as examples of excellence may still not survive. Within three years of the publication of *In Search of Excellence*, Hickman and Silva (1985) pointed out that three of the US firms included for their success had run into financial problems. The most worrying feature of this approach is its inconsistency over time. Within three years of publishing *In Search of Excellence*, Peters had published *A Passion for Excellence* (Peters and Austin, 1985). This gives a new view of management for success. It appeared just as Handy had published his adaptation of the now redundant version of excellence for teachers in the UK. Now management is reduced to MBWA, Management By Wandering Around. It is 'common sense', 'A Blinding Flash of the Obvious'. In the same year, *Creating Excellence* (Hickman and Silva, 1985) included a very different formula for success, with a heavy emphasis on strategy plus culture as the key. By 1988 both Peters (1987) and Waterman (1988) had changed the tune. Now corporate culture, the key point in the earlier book, was a threat to the innovation needed as markets changed quickly. To meet the competition, firms had to be masters of renewal to face the one constant in their situation, change. Within five years the definition of excellence had been changed. But the goalposts kept on moving. In 1989 Peters was writing that 'our so recently tried-and-true (yet still recent) management tools are, arguably, worthless, downright dangerous' (Peters, 1989). Yet he had already re-designed them thrice across the 1980s.

There is a final caution about this popular approach to management. The writers and those who use the evidence not only use a brash language, but suffer no modesty in their recommendations. As an antidote we turn to the father of American management study, Peter Drucker, born in 1909 and author of some twenty-two books on the subject. To Drucker (1987), claiming to have educated the Japanese about management and innovation, everything in *In Search of Excellence* was in his work published thirty years earlier. This may sound arrogant, but to Drucker, management is a discipline but not a science. It is a liberal art, focused one way on the culture and structure of the organisation and the other way on the results achieved. To him, the 'excellence' studies were superficial.

The implications for school management

The 'excellence' studies, especially when taken with the evidence on school effectiveness, provide valuable checklists for considering management in education. There is not, however, any blueprint that can be applied. The reasons for this are partly in the differences between schools and other organisations. Peters' 1987 book is titled *Thriving on Chaos*, which schools find difficult. But they also come from the nature of the evidence itself. It changes too fast for confidence. It is however possible to extract factors that appear so regularly in studies of industry and of schools that it would be foolish to ignore them. *In Search of Excellence* lists seven key features of organisation that seem to contribute to success. Waterman (1988) lists another eight. Each set overlaps with the factors from school effectiveness studies reported in Chapter 5.

The changes in the characteristics of effective firms identified by both Peters and Waterman in 1982 and in 1987 and 1988 are towards less certainty. By the end of the decade as the first 'excellent' firms ran into trouble, the key features tended to be stated as alternatives such as direction and empowerment, friendly facts and congenial controls, teamwork and politics, stability in motion, causes and commitment (Waterman, 1988). Using this approach produces a list of reminders of factors that should be considered when reviewing or changing the organisation. This aide-memoire is as follows.

Structure and culture – look at organisation, but also at relations.

Direction and empowerment – lead, but encourage others to take initiatives.

High expectations and user friendliness – set standards, but carry people with you.

Clarify and listen – set clear objectives, but welcome criticism.

Internal and external – carry staff with you, but also pupils and parents.

By now there is an obvious question about all this evidence. If these are the important factors, why is it so difficult to put them into practice, why have so many firms using these management techniques gone bankrupt or been taken over? Why, as they are so obvious, is so much fuss being made about them? The answer to all these questions is that the simple factors recommended for consideration in these studies are often neglected. Life is often too rushed for deliberation. The sceptic in me once suggested that if a school had the characteristics listed, it would be crazy to want it to change it (Shipman 1974). The exercise of checking structure and culture, top-down and bottom-up, internal and external is always worthwhile, whether there is calm or crisis. It is easy to think that a school is doing well if it is running smoothly. But performance is necessary as well as comfort. That requires a few hard questions.

12 Managing schools into the 21st century

The theme of this book is that school management has been deflected from learning. That has led, not only to a confusion of means with ends, but attention to procedures to be applied rather than developments to be encouraged. It is around learning that teachers are inspired to develop education. By concentrating school management on top-down procedures, training has missed both the opportunity to help teachers raise standards and to use their interest in helping children learn. That is particularly unfortunate given the stress in the 1988 Education Reform Act on raising attainment. That was an opportunity to re-focus management training on to learning. It was also an opportunity to align training to the enterprise assumed in the Act. It was an opportunity to involve parents. The timing was perfect. By the late 1980s, management literature outside education was stressing not only the importance of vision at the top, but of the need to encourage initiative at all levels of the organisation. Yet there is still no sign of any shift around management training in education. The stress is still on means confused with ends and on administration not management.

In this chapter questions are provided as an antidote to books and courses that reduce schooling to routine. The assumption behind these questions is that schooling is funded primarily to raise attainment through improving the conditions for learning. That requires a management style that encourages teachers to take initiatives, to feel that they have support for developing the curriculum and the way they organise learning. That is the message from studies of management reported in Chapter 10. Success comes from the efforts of those involved at all levels. They have to be informed and feel empowered. All teachers are managers. All must be in a position to lead.

Learning however is a responsibility for parents and pupils as well as teachers. That view is supported by the available evidence and is the assumption behind many of the developments in schools that are continually initiated by teachers. Giving learners more information on their progress, negotiating personal targets, shortening the time-span of assessments, contracting and negotiation are attempts to give children responsibilities. Informing and involving parents in the learning is also in line with the evidence. The 1988 Education Reform Act shares that emphasis on the importance of information and its availability, particularly on the progress of children through the curriculum. Legislation and bottom-up initiatives point to the need for school management to focus on learning and share not just information but responsibility for it.

The conclusions that follow may seem subversive. That is because the implementation of the 1988 Act will not take place in an unchanging world. That was the message of Chapter 3. Teachers will have to keep developing the curriculum. School management should encourage them. Indeed, the emphasis on leadership reported in Chapter 5 was partly about the importance of setting and sharing goals and partly about listening to the ideas of others. Teachers, pupils and parents are living in a changing world. They are the source of new initiatives. When a tough decision has to be made in school, or a course is dragging or a book becoming wearisome, these questioning conclusions can serve as a stimulant and *aide-memoire*. They ensure that ends are not confused with means, that the latter include the available evidence and that those involved are actively working out their own ways to move forward together.

What should be the content of school management training?

There are two approaches to learning that could add to the content of school management training in the direction required. One is to deal directly with topics immediately related to attainment. The second is to alter the content of existing topics in management training to give priority to topics related to learning.

Directly related topics

These should concentrate on factors identified in the evidence presented in Chapters 5, 6 and 7. This evidence is not merely academic. It has been honed in public debate and the idiosyncratic has been weeded out. It should be used in school management training. So should the copious literature supplied by HMI.

The Curriculum from 5 to 16 is itself an agenda for a learning-based training, especially when supplemented by its accompanying subject issues in the same *Curriculum Matters* series (DES, 1985). Examples of areas currently given too low a priority include the following.

- The context for learning – concentrating on the school as an environment in which teachers and children should have the maximum opportunity and support.
- The resources for learning – concentrating on the teacher and material resources inside and outside the school.
- Elements of learning – where the national curriculum has disturbed the balance between knowledge, concepts, skills and attitudes.
- Teaching styles – concentrating not only on individual pedagogy, but on the coordination of styles across the school.
- Responsibilities for learning – concentrating on policies for involving pupils and parents as well as teachers in negotiating targets, contracts and roles.
- Entitlement – concentrating on achieving a broad and balanced curriculum for all children through efficient monitoring and management.
- Assessment in learning – concentrating on the way assessment can be used to inform, direct and motivate in learning.
- The characteristics of the curriculum as defined by HMI (DES, 1985a).

This last topic is an example where curriculum is directly related to children's learning. The publication of the *Curriculum Matters* series provided an agenda for a review that linked the characteristics of the curriculum to elements of learning. The introduction of a National Curriculum reinforces the importance of that analysis. The information collected will enable the curriculum to be scrutinised and coordinated.

HMI listed the following characteristics of the curriculum that were necessary for all children to engage in a comparable range of learning.

Breadth including aesthetic and creative, human and social, linguistic and literary, mathematical, moral, physical, scientific, spiritual and technological. While overtaken by the National Curriculum, this breadth is still endorsed as a priority following the Act (see for example DES, 1989b).

Balance to ensure that the areas of learning above are each given time to be fully developed.

Relevance so that pupils see their needs being met.

Differentiation to allow for differences among children.

Progression to build on the existing knowledge of the child and ensure that demands are pitched to enable progress to be sustained.

Continuity to ensure that children do not feel lost as they go through school or transfer to another.

These characteristics of the curriculum were related to four elements of learning, knowledge, concepts, skills and attitudes. This analysis remains an important *aide-memoire* as staff consider the implementation of the national curriculum. Questions of pacing and sequencing children still remain important. Indeed, if entitlement is to mean anything this relation between curriculum and individual learning has to be put on the agenda.

The focus of existing topics
The conventional subjects of school management training are rarely treated as means to improving learning. This also applies to post-1988 courses such as the local management of schools, the National Curriculum and relations with governors and parents. Like the first wave of books on these subjects, the emphasis has been on procedure rather than purpose. Other subjects arising from the 1988 Education Reform Act have still to be given attention. An example is the organisation of information discussed in Chapters 8 and 9. With the overlapping packaging produced by the 1988 Education Reform Act reported in Chapter 2, any topics in the resourcing and political areas must be related to the curriculum and learning. The key to management is in the availability of information to all concerned, at all levels. That is the subject of Chapters 8 and 9. It is spelled out in documents on the Act (see for example DES, 1989). But it has

yet to enter management training.

The reorientation of existing courses to focus on learning is particularly important where there is pressure to act fast, but where there is insufficient information. The most obvious example is assessment. As National Curriculum assessment, including records of achievement, is built into the work of schools it will need to be synchronised with existing continuous assessment by teachers. Indeed, the national assessment is supposed to be primarily by teacher assessment, adjusted against Standard Assessment Tasks and moderated. Many in-service courses are being organised to help teachers insert this national assessment into existing arrangements. In secondary schools that includes GCSE and in many cases records of achievement. But the principles and procedures are still being trialled nationally and schools can obtain only limited advice on how they should be adjusting. The development work is likely to continue after schools have the arrangements in place as the century ends. It is difficult to move forward confidently. Yet the intention of the National Curriculum assessments is to raise standards by giving teachers, pupils and parents more information. That is certain. The principles agreed by the Secretary of State are that it should be formative, criterion-referenced, related to progression as well as moderated. The danger is that the effort to install the system will exhaust energy that should go to building the information into learning.

The same danger exists as teacher appraisal, staff development, school review, public relations, budgeting and marketing are organised. In-service training helps to get procedures into place, but in each case the procedures can lose their point. The objective is to help staff raise standards and increase support for this outside the school. The danger is even present in courses intended to help teachers secure the entitlement of specified groups of children, whether identified by sex, or race, or class, or special needs, to a broad and balanced education. The mechanics are so time-consuming that their implementation can become the goal.

Given the tendency for means to be confused with ends, here are questions that should be asked of all courses, books, articles and circulars from LEA and DES.

Question 1 What has this got to do with children learning? This question is an antidote to the confusion of means and ends in school management.

Question 1a   How strong is the culture for learning?
From the available evidence there should be

- *emphasis* on learning as the priority
- *high expectations* of standards to be achieved.

Question 1b   How effective is the structure of learning?
From the available evidence there should be

- *planning* to ensure that good practice is implemented
- *assessment* that informs teacher, pupil and parent.

These questions arise from the evidence presented in Chapters 5, 6 and 7. Learning is most likely in a climate of high expectations, agreement over the objectives and coursework and homework that is set, assessed and fed-back consistently. These aspects must be high on the agenda for management. They must be the subject of review. They do not stop in the classroom. They involve parents and the community as well as the teachers. The pupils too must feel that there is a warm yet stretching working environment. That has to be organised. It requires stability and order. All these factors stressed by researchers into effectiveness are present in the recommendations of the Elton Report on discipline in school (DES, 1989c). They stress the importance of the 'feel' of the school, of the emphasis on work, on rewards for achievement and on mutual support among teachers.

Question 2   What has this got to do with empowering people?
This question is an antidote to management that is over-concerned with procedures rather than people.

Question 2a   Is there a culture of empowerment?
From the available evidence there should be

- *emphasis* on the importance of bottom-up enterprise
- *high expectations* that teachers, pupils and parents will collaborate in developments.

Question 2b   Is there a structure for empowerment?
From the available evidence there should be

- *planning* to secure resources for developments and their integration into the mainstream of the school

- *appraisal* to ensure that responsibilities as well as rights are known.

These questions arise from the evidence in Chapters 5, 6 and 10. Management works through people. It should encourage leadership at all levels. That is particularly important in periods of rapid change. It is not just curriculum development that is a social process rather than an event. Success for the education service depends on nearly half a million teachers working in 20,000 schools, leading the way on curriculum and teaching style. In turn it depends on them working with pupils and their parents. With millions of people involved there has to be priority to making them feel that their efforts are important and a structure that enables them to be effective. Legislation cannot raise standards. Like school management it can only help create conditions where individuals are encouraged to do the job.

This emphasis on the importance of leadership and empowerment takes me back to my perambulating headteacher with the odd socks. He was leading from the front and sharing his passion for learning as he pottered around. Listening and empowering do not remove the responsibility to lead. That comes top of any list of factors in good management or school effectiveness. Leadership depends on being responsive to available information. That accounts for the success of MBWA, Management by Wandering Around. That is how new ideas are picked up and old ones seen to be redundant. It is how colleagues are encouraged and their efforts appraised. The evidence from studies of excellence in organisations points to leaders providing a clear sense of mission, clear objectives that enable all staff to lead. They are decisive, yet visible and approachable.

That need for balance is the primary message of studies of management. They emphasise apparently opposed factors, loose and tight, cultural and structural, leadership and empowerment, high expectations and attention to detail, rights and responsibilities. That is why it is difficult to lay down a blueprint for the development of schools. The balance serves as a reminder of factors that have to be considered before taking action. It does not map out the way forward. Management is about leadership because each alternative requires decisions at all levels, and that depends on establishing a clear, shared vision of the priorities for the school.

This raises a crucial question following the 1988 Education Reform Act. Will the National Curriculum, its accompanying tests and the changes in the responsibilities of school management be subject to progressive adaptation? Certainly the combination of national programmes of work, attainment targets and tests is a powerful constraint. These proposals were bitterly opposed. But the Act left implementation, the way the core and foundation subjects are to be arranged into a curriculum and taught, to teachers. They also choose the subjects for the remainder of the curriculum, allocate time to each subject and decide how each is to be taught. They will determine a distinctive image for their school. All the time they will adapt to further changes in the world outside the school.

The necessity to keep developing education to meet the changing needs of the population around schools in very different areas places a duty on teachers to implement the 1988 Education Reform Act in an active not passive way. The Act is designed to allow this to happen. For example, LEAs and governing bodies wanting a school to experiment can apply for an exception to the National Curriculum to be allowed. Governments depend on teachers to put legislation into practice. Teachers are experts in adapting government policies to fit local conditions. That was the message of Chapter 4.

There are usually three stages in converting policies handed down from above into practices in the classroom.

Stage 1 – Adaptation
Here teachers take the development and make marginal amendments to protect learning from excessively rapid change. Placed in an open-planned primary school, with advice that this meant the end of class teaching, most teachers moved about bookcases, screens and cupboards until they could live with the new architecture. Day-by-day the teaching styles were tentatively adapted to fit the new conditions. Soon, these changes had softened the initial radicalism of the new situation.

Stage 2 – Domestication
As time went by, screens, potted plants, creepers, paintings and papier maché sculptures appeared, making the place look like home.

Windows in particular were decorated until seeing in was reduced as in a conventional classroom. More important, the teachers settled on a pedagogy that was familiar and comfortable for them and for pupils and parents. This usually meant returning to class teaching but using the opportunities in the newly enclosed spaces.

Stage 3 – Subversion

By the time inspectors came round to look at the way the new policy of open-planned schooling was working the teachers had subverted it. In some cases they had gone back to classroom teaching as if nothing had happened. In other schools, learning had been reorganised to use the more open spaces. But those who wrote the Plowden Report must have wondered what happened to all those innovatory schools they used as examples of good practice. The answer lies in the staged accommodation of policies into the realities of classroom life. That is why the focal point for school management is where bottom-up developments meet top-down policies. That is where leadership is exercised.

Sometimes the pressure to implement in ways that are not amenable is too strong to resist. That is the case with many aspects of the 1988 Education Reform Act. But the adaptive and if necessary subversive power of half a million teachers should not be under-estimated. They have the local information. Against the advice of inspectors they converted secondary modern schools to public examinations in the 1950s and primary schools to mixed ability grouping in the 1970s. Often headteachers were in the lead. Grass-roots initiatives do not cease when top-down reforms are imposed. Just as electorates swing like a pendulum despite the efforts of politicians, so teachers make individual decisions and collectively move the service in radical ways. It often takes time to detect these changes. By then it is usually too late to stop them.

These bottom-up changes are not just reactions. They are attempts to implement national policies in the context of these children in this school, in this area. That is why headteachers take the lead. That is also what empowerment means. Action by teachers is a necessary condition for securing the attainment of children within the national framework now in place. Nothing in school management training should inhibit that initiative. Adaptation, domestication, even subversion are duties for concerned teachers.

References

Abel-Smith, B. and Townsend, P. (1965) *The Poor and the Poorest*. London: Bell.

Adams, N. (1989) 'Climate of Trust'. *Times Educational Supplement*, 17 February, p B5.

Anderson, D. (1987) 'A Prime Case of Myopia'. *Times*, 11 November, p 7.

Armstrong, M. (1980) *Closely Observed Children*. London: Chameleon Books.

Ashton, P. (1975) *The Aims of Primary Education*. Basingstoke: Macmillan.

Ausubel, D.P. (1963) *The Psychology of Meaningful Verbal Learning*. New York: Grune and Stratton.

Ball, S.J. (1987) *The Micro-Politics of the School*. London: Methuen.

Barker Lunn, J. (1982) 'Junior schools and their organizational policies', *Educational Research*, Vol. 24, No 4, pp 250–261.

Bassey, M. (1978) *Nine Hundred Primary School Teachers*. Windsor: NFER-Nelson.

Bastiani, J. (1987) *Parents and Teachers*. Windsor: NFER-Nelson.

Becher, T. et al. (1981) *Policies for Educational Accountability*. London: Heinemann.

Bell, L.A. (1980) 'The school as an organisation: a re-appraisal', *Brit. Jrn. of Soc. of Ed.* Vol. 1, No 2, pp 183–192.

Bennett, S.N. (1976) *Teaching Styles and Pupil Progress*. London: Open Books.

Bennett, S.N. et al. (1980) *Open Plan Schools: Teaching, Curriculum and Design*. Windsor: NFER-Nelson.

Bennett, S.N. et al. (1984) *The Quality of Pupil Learning Experiences*. Hillsdale, NJ: Erlbaum.

Berman, P. and McLaughlin, M.W. (1978) '*Federal Programs Supporting Educational Change*', *viii: Implementing and Sustaining Innovations*. Santa Monica: Rand Corp.

Best, R. et al (1983) *Education and Care: the study of a school and its pastoral organisation*. London: Heinemann.

Beveridge, W. (1942) *Social Insurance and Allied Services*. London: HMSO.

Blatchford, R. (ed.) (1985) *Managing the Secondary School.* London: Bell and Hyman.

Bloom, B.S. (1976) *Human Characteristics and School Learning.* New York: McGraw Hill.

Boydell, D. (1981) 'Classroom Organization 1970–7', in Simon, B. and Willcocks, J. (eds.) *Research and Practice in the Primary School Classroom.* London: Routledge and Kegan Paul.

Brown, M. (1971) 'Some strategies used in primary schools for initiating and implementing change'. *Unpublished M.Ed. thesis*, University of Manchester.

Brunt, M.P. (1987) 'Marketing Schools', in Craig, I. *Primary School Management in Action*, Harlow: Longman.

Burgess, R.G. (1983) *Experiencing Comprehensive Education: A Study of Bishop McGregor School.* London: Methuen.

Burgess, R.G. (1986) *Sociology, Education and Schools.* London: Batsford.

Bush, T. (1986) Theories of Educational Management. London: Harper and Row.

Caldwell, B.J. and Spinks, J.M. (1985) *The Self-Managing School.* Lewes: Falmer.

Campbell, R.J. (1985) *Developing the Primary School Curriculum.* Eastbourne: Holt, Rinehart and Winston.

Clifford, D.K. and Cavanagh, R.E. (1985) *The Winning Performance.* London: Sidgwick and Jackson.

Clough, E.E. et al. (1884) *Assessing Pupils.* Windsor: NFER-Nelson.

Coates, R. and Silburn, R. (1970) *Poverty: the Forgotten Englishman.* Harmondsworth: Penguin.

Cooper, R. (1988) *Management Development for the Extension of TVEI.* Cardiff: TVEI Unit.

Coopers and Lybrand (1988) *Local Management of Schools.* London: HMSO.

Cox, C.B. and Dyson, A.E. (eds) (1969) *A Black Paper.* London: The Critical Quarterly Society.

Crossman, R. (1969) *Paying for the Social Services.* London: Fabian Society.

Davies, B. and Braund, C. (1989) *Local Management of Schools.* Plymouth: Northcote House.

Day, C. et al. (1986) *Managing Primary Schools.* London: Harper and Row.

Department of Education and Science (1967) *Children and their Primary Schools.* London: HMSO.

Department of Education and Science (1974) *A Framework for Expansion.* London: HMSO.

Department of Education and Science (1977a) *Curriculum 11 to 16.* London: HMSO.

Department of Education and Science (1977b) *Ten Good Schools.* London: HMSO.

Department of Education and Science (1978) *Primary Education in England and Wales.* London: HMSO.

Department of Education and Science (1979) *Aspects of Secondary Education.* London: HMSO.

Department of Education and Science (1984) *Education Observed: A Review of the first six months of published reports.* London: HMSO.

Department of Education and Science (1985a) *The Curriculum from 5 to 16.* London: HMSO.

Department of Education and Science (1985b) *Better Schools.* London: HMSO.

Department of Education and Science (1986) *Better Schools: Evaluation and Appraisal.* London: HMSO.

Department of Education and Science (1987) *School Teachers' Pay and Conditions.* London: HMSO.

Department of Education and Science (1988) *National Curriculum: Task Group on Assessment and Testing: Report.* London: HMSO.

Department of Education and Science (1989a) *Records of Achievement.* London: HMSO.

Department of Education and Science (1989b) *From Policy to Practice.* London: HMSO.

Department of Education and Science (1989c) *Draft Circular: Charges for School Activities.* London: HMSO.

Department of Education and Science (1989d) *Discipline in Schools.* London: HMSO.

Douglas, J.W.B. (1964) *The Home and the School.* London: McGibbon and Kee.

Drucker, P. (1986) *The Frontiers of Management.* London: Heinemann.

Edwards, J. and Batley, R. (1978) *The Politics of Positive Discrimination.* London: Tavistock.

Emerson, C. and Goddard, I. (1989) *All About the National Curriculum.* London: Heinemann.

Everard, K.B. (1982) *Management in Comprehensive Schools – What can be learned from industry?* York: Centre for the Study of Comprehensive Schools.

Everard, K.B. (1986) *Developing Management in Schools.* Oxford: Blackwell.

Felsenstein, D. (1987) *Comprehensive Achievement.* London: Hodder and Stoughton.

Fullan, M. (1982) *The Meaning of Educational Change.* New York: Teachers College Press.

Galton, M. and Simon, B. (1980) *Progress and Performance in the Primary Classroom*. London: Routledge and Kegan Paul.

Gipps, C. and Goldstein, H. (1983) *Testing Children*. London: Heinemann.

Glennerster, H. and Wilson, G. (1970) *Paying for Private Schools*. London: Allen Lane.

Goffman, I. (1961) *Asylums*. New York: Anchor.

Goldsmith, W. and Clutterbuck, D. (1982) *The Winning Streak*. London: Weidenfeld and Nicolson.

Gray, J. and Hannon, V. (1985) *HMI's Interpretations of Schools' Examination Results*. Division of Education: University of Sheffield.

Handy, C. (1984) *Taken for Granted: looking at schools as organizations*. London: Longman.

Hargreaves, D.H. (1967) *Social Relations in a Secondary School*. London: Routledge and Kegan Paul.

Halsey, A.H. (1978) *Change in British Society*. Oxford: Oxford University Press.

Harris, R. and Seldon, A. (1979) *Overruled on Welfare*. London: Institute of Economic Affairs.

Hearnshaw, L.S. (1979) *Cyril Burt: Psychologist*. London: Hodder and Stoughton.

Hickman, C.R. and Silva, M.A. (1985) *Creating Excellence*. London: Unwin.

Holt, M. (1987) *Judgement, Planning and Educational Change*. London: Harper and Row.

House of Commons Expenditure Committee (1976) *Policy Making in the Department of Education and Science*. London: HMSO.

Hurman, A. (1978) *A Charter for Choice*. Windsor: NFER-Nelson.

Hurt, J.S. (1979) *Elementary Schooling and the Working Classes, 1860–1918*. London: Routledge and Kegan Paul.

Inner London Education Authority (1983) *Race, Class and Sex 1. Achievement in Schools*. London: ILEA.

International School Improvement Project (1986) *Report*. Paris: Organisation for Economic Co-operation and Development.

Jackson, P.W. (1968) *Living in Classrooms*. New York: Holt, Rinehart and Winston.

Kysel, F. (1982) *Study of pre-school experience*. London: ILEA.

Lacey, C. (1970) *Hightown Grammar*. Manchester: Manchester University Press.

Lindsay, K. (1926) *Social Progress and Educational Waste*. London: Routledge.

McCann, P. (1977) *Popular Education and Socialization in the Nineteenth Century*. London: Methuen.

McMahon, A. and Bolam, R. (1987) *School Management Development*.

A Handbook for LEAs. Bristol: National Development Centre for School Management Training.

Manzer, R.A. (1970) *Teachers and Politics.* Manchester: Manchester University Press.

Morgan, G. (1986) *Images of Organization.* Beverley Hills: Sage.

Mortimore, J. and Blackstone, T. (1981) *Disadvantage in Education.* London: Heinemann.

Mortimore, P. et al. (1988) *School Matters.* Wells: Open Books.

Musgrove, F. (1971) *Patterns of Power and Authority in English Education.* London: Methuen.

National Foundation for Educational Research (1987) *The TVEI Experience.* Sheffield: Manpower Services Commission.

National Foundation for Educational Research (1989) *The Search for Success.* Slough: NFER.

Organization for Economic Cooperation and Development (1975) *Educational Development Strategy in England and Wales.* Paris: OECD.

Office of Population Censuses and Surveys (1988) *Social Trends.* London: HMSO.

Oldroyd, D. and Caldwell, B.J. (1988) *Local Financial Management and the Self-Managing School: Perspectives and Practices.* Bristol: National Development Centre for School Management Training.

Ozga, J. (1988) *Schoolwork. Approaches to the Labour Process of Teaching.* Milton Keynes: Open University Press.

Peters, T. (1987) *Thriving on Chaos.* London: MacMillan.

Peters, T. (1989) 'Tomorrow's Companies'. *Economist,* 4–10 March, pp 27–30.

Peters, T. and Austin, N. (1985) *A Passion for Excellence.* London: Collins.

Peters, T. and Waterman, R.J. (1982) *In Search of Excellence.* New York: Harper and Row.

Pukey, S.C. and Smith, M.S. (1983) Effective Schools: a review. *Elementary School Journal,* 83:4.

Reid, K., Hopkins, D. and Holley, P. (1987) *Towards the Effective School.* Oxford: Blackwell.

Roethlisberger, F.J. and Dickson, W.J. (1939) *Management and the Worker.* New York: Wiley.

Rutter, M. et al. (1979) *Fifteen Thousand Hours.* London: Open Books.

Sarason, S.B. (1982) *The Culture of the School and the Problem of Change.* Boston: Allyn and Bacon.

Schools Council (1979) *Impact and Take-up Project.* London: Schools Council.

Schools Council (1981) *The Practical Curriculum*. London: Schools Council.

Shipman, M.D. (1971) 'Innovation in Schools', in Walton, J. (ed.) *Curriculum Organization and Design*. London: Ward Lock.

Shipman, M.D. (1974) *Inside a Curriculum Project*. London: Methuen.

Shipman, M.D. (1978) *In-School Evaluation*. London: Heinemann.

Shipman, M.D. (1980) 'The Limits of Positive Discrimination', in Marland, M. *Education for the Inner City*. London: Heinemann, pp 69–94.

Shipman, M.D. (1984) *Education as a Public Service*. London: Harper and Row.

Shipman, M.D. (1985) *The Management of Learning in the Classroom*. London: Hodder and Stoughton.

Shipman, M.D. (1988) *The Limitations of Social Research (3rd ed)*. Harlow: Longman.

Shipman, M.D. and Cole, H. (1975) 'Educational indices in the allocation of resources', *Secondary Education*, Vol 5, No 2, pp 37–8.

Simon, H. (1945) *Administrative Behaviour*. New York: MacMillan.

Southgate, V. et al. (1981) *Extending Beginning Reading*. London: Heinemann.

Stanworth, M. (1983) *Gender and Schooling*. London: Hutchinson.

Statistical Information Services (1988) *Performance Indicators for Schools*. London: Chartered Institute of Public Finance and Accountancy.

Stenner, A. (1987) 'School-centred financial management', in Craig, I. (ed), *Primary School Management in Action*. Harlow: Longman, pp 69–80.

Taylor, F.W. (1911) *Scientific Management*. New York: Harper.

Taylor, G. and Ayres, N. (1969) *Born and Bred Unequal*. London: Longman.

Thomas, H. (1988) 'Pupils as vouchers', *Times Educational Supplement*, 2 December, p 23.

Tizard, B. et al. (1988) *Young Children at School in the Inner City*. Hove: Erlbaum.

Tizard, B. and Hughes, M. (1984) *Young Children Learning*. London: Fontana.

Tomlinson, J. (1984) *Home and School in Multicultural Britain*. London: Batsford.

Topping, K. and Wolfendale, S. (1985) *Parental Involvement in Children's Reading*. Beckenham: Croom Helm.

Turner, G. and Clift, P.S. (1985) 'Teachers' perceptions of a voluntary LEA scheme for school self-evalution', Educational Research, Vol 27, No 2, pp 127–41.

Waterman, R.H. (1988) *The Renewal Factor.* London: Bantam.

Weiss, C.H. (1982) 'Policy Research in the Context of Diffuse Decision-Making', in Kallen, D.B.P. et al., *Social Science Research and Public Policymaking.* Windsor: NFER-Nelson.

Woods, P. (1976) 'Having a laugh: an antidote to schooling', in Hammersley, M. and Woods, P. (eds.) *The Process of Schooling.* London: Routledge and Kegan Paul.

Woods, P. (1980) *The Divided School.* London: Routledge and Kegan Paul.

Index